LinkedIn®
WORK FOR YOU

A Practical Handbook for Lawyers and Other Legal Professionals

Dennis Kennedy
Allison C. Shields

TABLE OF CONTENT

ABOUT THE AUTHORS

DENNIS KENNEDY (dmk@denniskennedy.com) is President of Dennis Kennedy Advisory Services LLC, an information technology and innovation lawyer, and author well-known for promoting the use of technology in the practice of law. He focuses on innovation, legal technology, speaking, writing, and coaching and is an adjunct professor in the LegalRnD program at Michigan State University College of Law and also at the University of Michigan Law School. Dennis retired as Senior Counsel for the Digital Payments & Labs group at Mastercard, where he focused on information technology law, fintech law and innovation. His new company will concentrate on innovation, legal technology and productization, including "Legal Innovation as a Service" packages and the Kennedy Idea Propulsion Laboratory. Dennis is a Fellow of the College of Law Practice Management and former chair of the board of the American Bar Association's Legal Technology Resource Center. Dennis wrote the legal technology column for the ABA Journal for many years, has authored and co-authored several books, including *Successful Innovation Outcomes in Law: A Practical Guide for Law Firms, Law Departments, and Legal Organizations* (2019), *The Lawyer's Guide to Collaboration Tools and Technologies:*

Smart Ways to Work Together (2nd edition, 2018) with Tom Mighell, and *LinkedIn in One Hour for Lawyers* and *Facebook in One Hour for Lawyers*, with Allison Shields. He co-hosts The Kennedy-Mighell Report podcast on the Legal Talk Network, and has written his blog, DennisKennedy.Blog, since 2003. On Twitter, Dennis may be found at @denniskennedy and was one of the earliest lawyers with a website (1995). LinkedIn: ***www.linkedin.com/in/dennismkennedy***

ALLISON C. SHIELDS (Allison@LegalEaseConsulting.com) is the President of Legal Ease Consulting, Inc., where she coaches lawyers on practice management, productivity and business development issues, including how to use social networking effectively as a marketing tool. She is the author of the Legal Ease Blog (***www.legaleaseconsulting.com***) and the *Simple Steps* column in the American Bar Association Law Practice Division's *Law Practice* magazine. She is a former practicing lawyer, law firm manager, and administrative partner, as well as the former Executive Director of the Suffolk County Bar Association's Academy of Law. A nationally recognized speaker, Allison presents workshops and programs in both private and public settings. She is also the author of numerous published articles on practice management and business development/marketing topics. Her website, Lawyer Meltdown (**www.lawyermeltdown.com**), provides resources and information for lawyers about managing and building their practices. She is the coauthor, with Dennis Kennedy, of *LinkedIn in One Hour for Lawyers* and *Facebook in One Hour for Lawyers*, and with Daniel Siegel of *How to Do More in Less Time: The Complete Guide to Increasing Your Productivity and Improving Your Bottom Line*. You can find Allison on Twitter @allisonshields and on LinkedIn at **https://www.linkedin.com/in/allisoncshieldslegalease.**

ACKNOWLEDGMENTS

We want to acknowledge and thank all of our colleagues, friends, clients, attendees of our presentations and webinars, readers of our other LinkedIn books and articles, those who have asked us to write or speak about LinkedIn, and our many LinkedIn Connections for their support, their interest in LinkedIn, and their questions and comments over the years that have helped us to learn more, experiment more, and continue refining our LinkedIn strategies and approaches. Grace Kennedy helped with proofreading and contributed the Foreword and Chapter 27. And a big thank you again to our families for their patience, understanding, and support during the book process, and the rest of the time as well.

LinkedIn is a registered trademark of the LinkedIn Corporation.

FOREWORD

by Grace Kennedy

I started using LinkedIn at the suggestion of my dad, Dennis Kennedy. He, along with Allison Shields, co-authored "LinkedIn® in One Hour for Lawyers" in 2013. Although the book was targeted at lawyers, I quickly learned that the suggestions in the book could benefit everyone, not just lawyers. I noticed that LinkedIn could also benefit a variety of people, and any generation could find value in what it could offer, whether the user was a boomer, millennial, gen X, gen Z, or what have you. LinkedIn can offer opportunities for anyone, regardless of age or experience level.

This book is a different book than their prior book for several reasons. It's more strategic and less how-to, although there's still a lot of great how-tos. The book is also less about lawyers and more about everyone in the legal industry. In my opinion, it applies to anyone outside the legal profession as well.

I learned so much from this book as I helped proofread it and make suggestions. I'm also grateful to get the opportunity to add a chapter from the millennial perspective. My dad tries his best, but he doesn't quite have the millennial perspective down.

You will learn a lot of great tips to grow your business, build your brand, and find the job you want from this book. Allison and my dad are great teachers. It's time to start reading and get to work.

INTRODUCTION

Lawyers and other legal professionals live and move in a world of interlocking, evolving networks of people. They connect on a daily basis with formal and informal networks of colleagues, clients, opposing counsel, service providers, experts, and others who are essential to the successful practice of law. They also use these connections to get referrals and recommendations, obtain information, move projects and cases forward, and assist their clients.

In contrast to other social media platforms, LinkedIn® emphasizes professional networking over personal interactions. Founded in 2003, LinkedIn passed one hundred million registered users in 2011 and, at the time of this writing, has zoomed past the six hundred thirty million mark, making it the premier business social networking tool today. One hundred seventy-four million users are in the United States. Three hundred three million users are active on LinkedIn each month, and forty percent of those use it daily.

A few more statistics: ninety million "senior-level influencers," sixty-three million "decision-makers," and ten million "C-level executives" have LinkedIn accounts. More than six million job openings are posted on LinkedIn each month. Hootsuite does a great job of collecting LinkedIn statistics at https://blog.hootsuite.com/linkedin-statistics-business/. For specific statistics on use in the legal profession, we like GreenTarget's annual "State of Digital Content Marketing Survey (*https://greentarget.com/wp-content/uploads/2019/07/Greentarget-2019-State-of-Digital-Content-Marketing-Survey-FINAL-7-25.pdf*). Among its many results is that only

29% of inhouse counsel agree that their outside law firms are using LinkedIn effectively.

We have found that even the lawyers and legal professionals most wary of social media will consider using LinkedIn. LinkedIn's universe of Profiles and Connections and its emphasis on professional relationships just make sense to those in the legal industry.

"Legal professionals" or "lawyers"—a note on usage.

In this book, we wanted to break down the barrier often seen in the legal profession between those who are lawyers and those working in the legal field who are not lawyers. We've made a concerted effort to use the inclusive term "legal professionals" and be precise about using the term "lawyer" in the appropriate context, as in the chapter on legal ethics. If we missed something, it's not for lack of trying.

Legal professionals often tell us that they barely use LinkedIn and would like to learn to use it better or more effectively than they do now. What they often mean is that they do not understand basic LinkedIn features, let alone strategies.

What's different about this book?

We have written a completely new version of our original book on LinkedIn for several reasons: the increasing use of LinkedIn by legal professionals, massive interface and feature changes in the LinkedIn service itself, and the positive reception we received to our first two LinkedIn books, and to our lectures and presentations about LinkedIn since we first presented on LinkedIn together in 2011.

We wanted the new book to reflect changes we've seen over the years, the lessons we have learned during that time from our own experience with LinkedIn, the feedback we have gotten from the books and our later articles and presentations about LinkedIn, and from our experience working with legal professionals and their use of LinkedIn. We also decided to publish this book direct to Kindle, rather than as a print publication.

Social media tools—including LinkedIn—can and do change often (and dramatically). As a cloud service, LinkedIn can update its features and interface on a regular basis, even overnight. In general, that is a good thing, as the service evolves to become more useful and to respond to user feedback. But it makes it difficult to release a print publication like the original book, containing lots of screenshots, because the book can become outdated very quickly. Over the past several years, we've seen LinkedIn make numerous dramatic changes, from its interface change in 2013 to changes following LinkedIn's purchase by Microsoft, adding and deleting features rapidly. As a result, we've decided not to include any screenshots in this book.

What are you hiring LinkedIn to do?

We like the approach originated by Clayton Christensen (author of *The Innovator's Dilemma* and other books and the person most commonly associated with the notion of "disruptive technologies"), known as the jobs-to-be-done framework. We have started to use it in our presentations and articles about LinkedIn.

In simplest terms, this approach asks and tries to answer the question: "What are you hiring LinkedIn to do?" Spending some time with this question can greatly enhance and clarify your approach to and use of LinkedIn. For example, if you are "hiring" LinkedIn to help you find a job, you will use it differently than if you are hiring LinkedIn to help you fill an open position. If you want to hire LinkedIn to find new local clients for your law practice, you will do something different than if you want to hire it to help you find speaking opportunities. Our sense is that **LinkedIn will work best for most lawyers and other legal professionals if they hire it to help them create, manage, and care for their network of referrers and potential referrers of business**. We invite you to keep that in mind as you read the book.

Bringing LinkedIn to the real world.

As we began to speak more often about LinkedIn, we found that we kept coming back to one point: LinkedIn works best when it overlaps with the real world. The most successful LinkedIn users seem to have a knack for using LinkedIn to supplement what they are already doing in the real world and using the real world to enhance what they are doing in LinkedIn. This cross-pollination does not have to be difficult or complex. Learning that a LinkedIn Connection has a new job can lead to a phone call or lunch invitation. Meeting someone at a conference can result in that person becoming a Connection. You can check LinkedIn when you visit another city to see what Connections you can meet in person. There is an organic element to LinkedIn networking; letting LinkedIn and the real world interact and overlap in simple ways can provide great benefits.

Before you dive into this book, we suggest you take a few minutes to think about how many people you talk to and work with in the average day or week. It might surprise you. If you map out on paper the people you know and your relationships in some of the categories we mentioned (e.g., colleagues, clients, providers), you will quickly see how rich and complex your networks can be, even if you are a solo practitioner.

If you then consider the ways in which your networks allow you to tap into the similar networks of your connections for recommendations and referrals, you will see the value of "who you know" and "who they know" in your professional practice. Legal professionals who do well for themselves, their clients, and those they work with often have long-standing, well-nurtured, and thriving networks.

LinkedIn is a tool to help you make your networks more visible and usable than they are when only in your head. It lets you map your networks, organize them, grow and nurture them, and efficiently use them both for your own benefit and the benefit of your connections. It does so in an easy-to-understand way that works very well for lawyers, with results you can see and measure.

The Three Essential Building Blocks

This book focuses on the three parts of your LinkedIn presence that you must understand well: Profiles, Connections, and Participation. We have long called these the essential building blocks of LinkedIn. In many ways, the three blocks notion is our fundamental insight in this book. If you understand and get these blocks right, you will "get" LinkedIn and should find it a valuable use of your time.

► Profiles establish your presence and professional identity on LinkedIn. Your Profile is an online, living professional biography or résumé that lets others know, in detail, who you are. Your Profile is your "face" on LinkedIn.

► Connections are the people in your networks. LinkedIn lets you identify people in your existing networks, find new people to meet, and invite them all to connect to you. By accepting these invitations, people show that they are connected professionally.

► Participation is the cultivating and tending of Connections in your network. It is the way you engage with members of your network. Legal professionals who have joined LinkedIn but say they have found no value often have neglected this crucial aspect. Properly understood, social media is participatory media. You must put effort into your online networking, just as you do your real-world networking.

How This Book is Organized

This book has six sections. You are welcome to read them in order or to dip into whatever topics interest you the most. We can see that you would keep the book at hand when you work on LinkedIn or do a periodic review of your LinkedIn strategies and results.

Section I covers getting off to a good start (or restart) on LinkedIn, including premium accounts, the mobile app, settings, and strategies.

Sections II, III and IV focus, respectively, on Profiles, Connections, and Participation.

Section V sets out a basic LinkedIn strategic plan that you can adapt and follow.

Section VI discusses some important specialty topics that will help you to truly make LinkedIn work for *you*, including personal branding, job searches, use by law students, moving to new locations or practice areas, using LinkedIn business tools (including Company Pages), legal ethics, use by Millennials and others new to the platform, resources, and when you need help.

There is no question that LinkedIn is currently, and likely will remain, the number one social networking tool for legal professionals. LinkedIn's emphasis on professional networking, and its alignment with the approach legal professionals prefer, make it well suited to lawyers' needs.

It is not just "who you know" literally that makes the biggest difference in the success of your practice, but how you create, nurture, and maintain a community of those whom you know. That is what LinkedIn offers, and this book will help you use it for those purposes.

Let's get started.

PART I

GETTING STARTED

1

SETTING UP A NEW ACCOUNT OR REVIVING YOUR EXISTING ACCOUNT

E ven though LinkedIn debuted in 2003 and has more than 600 million users as this book is written, it is not too late to get started. In fact, if you don't have a LinkedIn account, you can start right now and, by the time you finish this book, be among the best users of LinkedIn among legal professionals. Or, if you already have an account, you may be like so many legal professionals we speak with, and you never really done anything with it. Our goal is to change that. The first step starts with this chapter.

LinkedIn is an online service, not a software program. In fact, LinkedIn is a good example of cloud computing. There is no software to install, and you do not have to have a certain type of computer—just a PC or Mac, tablet device, or smartphone connected to the Internet. You can use LinkedIn anytime and anywhere you have Internet access.

In this short chapter, we will help you create or reactivate your LinkedIn account. The process is simple and familiar for anyone who has ever set up an online account. If you are already actively using your LinkedIn account or know that you have a working LinkedIn account that you can access even if you aren't actively using it, feel free to skip to the next chapter. On the other hand, it's a short chapter and there are a few tips, especially about email addresses, that might make a quick read of this chapter (or at least the tips section) worth your while.

Because there are more than 170 million LinkedIn users in the United States and you are reading this book, we feel safe in assuming it will be the rare reader who doesn't have a LinkedIn account and needs to set one up from scratch. Also, as long as you can access any existing LinkedIn account you have, we recommend reviving and rebuilding that account rather than starting up a new account.

Nonetheless, if you need to set up a new account, doing so is very easy and will be similar to setting up any other online account that you have.

Setting up a New LinkedIn Account

Go to *http://www.linkedin.com* and click on the "Join Now" button. Complete the registration form with your e-mail and a strong password. Your password must contain at least six characters. We highly recommend that it be unique to your LinkedIn account and be a "strong" password—twelve or more characters and a combination of uppercase and lowercase letters, numbers, and symbols. If you are not using a password manager, such as 1Password or LastPass, now would be a good time to get one and put your password into the manager. You might also consider letting the password manager generate a strong password for you. Then click on the "Agree and Join" button. You have the opportunity to review legal terms.

When you receive the confirming e-mail from LinkedIn (probably in a matter of seconds), follow the instructions to log in to your new account.

Accessing an Existing (and Probably Not Often Used) Account

In our experience, there are large numbers of people who set up a LinkedIn account, sometimes many years ago, and can no longer access it. The most common reason is that they have forgotten their passwords. If you don't use a password manager, you now have another reminder of why they are so useful.

People who have forgotten their LinkedIn passwords fall into two categories. The first group still has access to the email addresses (and, in some cases, phone numbers) they used to set up their accounts or the secondary addresses they provided to LinkedIn for their accounts. The second group does not. The second group has a harder job than the first group. However, we recommend that the second group try to restore and revive their existing account rather than create a new one.

No matter that group you are in, it's worth the effort to make a few educated guesses about what password you used when setting up the account. But just a few.

Your next step is to try to reset your password. Go to the LinkedIn website (***http://www.linkedin.com***) and attempt to sign in. You will see boxes to enter your e-mail address and password and a Sign In button. Highly visible below the Sign In button are the words "Forgot password?". Simply click on them and you will be taken to the password reset process.

The password reset process involves sending you an email to the email address associated with your account. Once you submit your address, LinkedIn will send you an e-mail with a link to a page where you can create a new password. Make it a strong password and promise us that you will either now remember it or store it securely in a password manager program. Once you can log in to your account, you are ready to use your account again.

It is possible that you started your LinkedIn account using an e-mail address you can no longer access (e.g., an e-mail address from a former law firm). In that case, the password reset option will not be available. Fortunately, LinkedIn gives you some other options to access your account. If you gave LinkedIn a phone number to associate with your account, that can be a big help.

Rather than walk you through the current options, which might change, we simply want to advise you to go to the LinkedIn Help pages, (found at ***https://www.linkedin.com/help/linkedin***), which are extensive and very, well, helpful. The Help sections on re-accessing your account when you don't have access to the original account are excellent and will walk you through the process. You can take comfort in not being the first or only person who has had this issue. As an aside, this procedure might be necessary for accessing an account after someone has become incapacitated or incompetent or has died.

Adding a secondary email address and phone number to your account ensures that you won't get locked out of your account if you change jobs and no longer have access to your old email account or phone number. You can log in to LinkedIn with any email address associated with your account. If you had a secondary email associated with your account, you could go to the login screen, enter your email address and then click on the Forgot password link to reset your password and gain access to your account. LinkedIn would send the necessary email to that secondary email address.

At the end of this process, you will either have access to your existing account or you will not. If you can get into your account, change the email address and password and you are ready to get started.

If you fail to get access, realistically you are looking at setting up a new account. We recommend that as a last resort only if you're absolutely certain that there is no way to access or eliminate the old account. Having two accounts in your name with partial information will only serve to cause confusion. In addition, LinkedIn's terms of use don't allow you to have multiple profiles. Once you've created the new Profile, you may need to contact LinkedIn to have the old Profile removed.

Tips

► Use a personal "permanent" email address (such as your Gmail account) in connection with your LinkedIn account, either as the primary account email or as a backup.

► Add a telephone number to your LinkedIn account as a backup.

► If you have a work email address associated with your LinkedIn account, change it while you still have access to the account if you are planning to leave your employer.

► Your password for your LinkedIn account should be different from every other password you use.

► Use a "strong" password (a combination of twelve or more uppercase and lowercase letters, numbers, and symbols) and a password manager application (1Password, KeePass, LastPass).

► Set up two-step verification (or multifactor authentication) on your LinkedIn account to keep it as secure as possible.

Choosing a Free or Premium Account

One of the most frequently asked questions we receive about LinkedIn is whether it is worth it to pay for one of LinkedIn's premium accounts. For most legal professionals, the basic (and free!) LinkedIn account will work well. And it has worked well for many years. You can be quite happy with the free service. However, there are a number of situations when a premium account might make good sense for you. Note that premium services can be used on a trial basis or on a "month-to-month" basis where you can start them and end them when you want, so there is very little risk in signing up for a premium account to try it out for a short time.

LinkedIn offers four types of premium accounts that currently range in cost from $24.99 to $99.95 per month (on annualized basis). LinkedIn also offers a number of customized premium services for enterprises, sales, and hiring. The customized services require engagement with LinkedIn salespeople and are priced in accordance with what you select.

We will focus on the four standard premium packages that can be purchased through LinkedIn without requiring direct contact with a LinkedIn salesperson—Premium Career, Premium Business, Sales Navigator Pro, and Recruiter Lite. These services are summarized in several places on the LinkedIn website. Rather than list the current features of each account (which, in our experience, are likely to keep changing), we encourage you to take a fresh look at what's available when you actually consider getting a premium account.

LinkedIn wants to make it easy for you to become a premium member. You may see a link in the top navigation bar to sign up for a free one-month trial of a premium account, or receive emails offering premium account trials.

Premium account owners enjoy enhanced features like details on who has viewed your Profile, analytics, education, and communications tools (such as additional LinkedIn InMail services that allow you to message people who are not Connections), and access to a variety of reports LinkedIn calls Insights. For example, with Premium Career, you can see where your Profile ranks among other candidates for the same job.

Here is a summary of the current benefits of the four premium account types:

Account Type	Premium Career	Premium Business	Sales Navigator Pro	Recruiter Lite
	$299.88* ($24.99 / month)	$575.88* ($47.99 / month)	$779.88* ($64.99 / month)	$1,199.40* ($99.95 / month)
InMail per month	5	15	20	30
Who's viewed your profile	☑	☑	☑	☑
Job insights	☑	☑	☑	☑
Salary insights	☑	☑	☑	☑
LinkedIn Learning	☑	☑	☑	☑
Business insights		☑	☑	☑
Unlimited people browsing		☑	☑	☑

Advanced search filters	☑	☑
Saved notes on Profiles	☑	☑
Additional sales and hiring tools	• Sales spotlights • Lead recommendations • Saved leads and accounts • Email integration	• Guided search • Smart suggestions • Saved search alerts • Projects

Choosing Between Premium Accounts

We have found that many job seekers get the Premium Career account during their job search and then turn it off when they obtain a job. It's that useful. A bit of a warning, though: the additional features are useful and you might not want to live without them, especially the "Who's viewed your Profile" feature, and you might not get around to turning the premium account off. The Premium Career account also allows you to turn on a feature only visible to recruiters that allows you to signal to recruiters (not your employer) that you are open to inquiries.

Many recruiting, marketing, business development, and sales people also use premium accounts on a regular basis. Often, their organization supplies the premium account to assist them in doing their jobs. The chart above and the additional materials and LinkedIn's "frequently asked questions" will help you make a decision. If you are interested in learning more about LinkedIn's different premium accounts and their features, we recommend that you search the Help section, or click on the link from your Home page to try Premium for free, which will bring you to a questionnaire to help you choose the right Premium plan for you.

We have heard many good reports on the Sales Navigator Pro account. Dennis recently switched over to this account in connection with launching some new services. This tool is especially good when you are looking to generate leads, build a sales pipeline, launch a new service, or promote an existing service. Users especially like the ability to do very granular searches on geography, job titles, and the like.

All of the premium accounts open the door to LinkedIn's educational materials, many of which grew out of its acquisition of Lynda.com, a well-known online education site. You simply click on the "Learning" icon on the top navigation bar of LinkedIn (in the web version) and you'll see the extent and variety of these learning resources. You can personalize your interests and then will be recommended relevant courses, popular courses, and suggested courses. You will find courses on big topics like management, marketing, and technology, and focused topics or skills like cloud computing, team-building, or executive coaching. Currently, there are more than 13,000 courses, with dozens added weekly. (If you have a free account, you can click the "Learning" icon under the "Work" tab on the navigation bar to get an idea of the kinds of courses that are offered, and to get a month for free).

Premium accounts also give you a great dashboard page, accessible to you from your LinkedIn homepage that summarizes the extra data and features you are getting from your specific premium account. We will mention some of the premium features throughout the book in places where they are relevant.

How to Upgrade to a Premium Account

Not surprisingly, LinkedIn makes it easy for you to upgrade to a premium account. Currently, the easiest way is click on the down arrow on the "Me" button on the top navigation bar of your LinkedIn homepage. There should be a small thumbnail photo of you there. On the dropdown menu, you find a selection for premium options. Click on it and explore.

Review the additional features and evaluate whether they make sense for you. A premium account might make sense for legal marketing professionals, during a hiring process, or during a job search (and LinkedIn has additional premium options in these categories), but the basic free account will be sufficient for most readers of this book. If you change your mind and want to upgrade later, it is easy to do so.

We expect LinkedIn to continue to roll out more premium features. Although we can't predict what those will be, we can suggest that you watch for new premium features and consider whether they might offer benefits for you in certain situations. And we also note that in the past, as LinkedIn has rolled out certain premium accounts and features, it has eliminated some of those features from free accounts, so it is possible that your free account in the future could lose some of its current functionality as LinkedIn tries to move more users to paid accounts.

Unless we note otherwise, the rest of this book will talk about what you can do with the basic free account.

2

USING LINKEDIN ON YOUR MOBILE DEVICES

The LinkedIn mobile app is excellent. And free. Download it from the Apple App Store or Google Play, install and use it on your smartphone and/or tablet device. Having access to information about people wherever you are is great, especially if you meet them at a conference or are meeting for lunch or coffee and want to have a photo of who you are looking for. And your train commute to work or downtime waiting in court or at a doctor's office are all excellent times to catch up with what is happening with your Network, send or accept invitations, or create short posts on LinkedIn through the app.

You won't be alone in using the LinkedIn mobile app. Fifty-seven percent of LinkedIn use is now on mobile.

You can find more information about the app at https://mobile.linkedin.com/. Here you will also find information about other stand-alone LinkedIn apps, which currently are LinkedIn Job Search; LinkedIn SlideShare (access more than 18 million SlideShare presentations); LinkedIn Learning (online courses); LinkedIn Recruiter; LinkedIn Sales Navigator; and LinkedIn Elevate (content sharing). Some of the apps (e.g., Sales Navigator) require the premium account associated with the tool.

In our experience, there are only a few minor differences between the LinkedIn app and the website/desktop version. These differences are disappearing and presumably will continue to do so. One difference that we highlight in our presentations is that, in some cases, the procedure for sending a personalized invitation to connect through the app is different than it is in the desktop version. It can be a surprise when you click to invite someone and expect to see a box for adding a personalized message and instead see a message that the invitation has already been sent. On the other hand, if you are using the mobile app to connect with someone standing in front of you at a conference, there is no need for a personalized message. You are likely to use both.

The mobile app has some great features for in-person connecting. The app has a built-in QR code scanner, and, as we will discuss later, you can easily create a QR code that someone can scan and be instantly sent to your LinkedIn Profile. Dennis has put the QR code for his LinkedIn profile on his paper business cards.

If you are at a conference or meeting, you can also turn on the "People Nearby" feature and see all of the people in the room who choose to participate and who are second degree connections. You can easily add them all as LinkedIn Connections. Some people are wary of this "broadcast" feature and turn it off but it can be a great tool to connect everyone at a small conference or retreat without the need for exchanging business cards.

The mobile app also allows you to get notifications of activities ("likes" of your posts, invitations, etc.). That can be a great way to keep getting the information even if you turn off the corresponding email alerts from LinkedIn.

We have seen the LinkedIn mobile app get better and better over the years. We expect to see that improvement continue. If you are not using the mobile app, you will definitely want to give it a try and not limit yourself to just the website/desktop version.

3

OPTIMIZING YOUR SETTINGS

I t is impossible to overstate the importance of choosing appropriate privacy and other settings in social media. You must understand your settings options and their implications. Accepting default settings in social media tools, including LinkedIn, simply means that you are choosing what is best for the company offering the tool, not what is best for you.

Although LinkedIn has had a better track record than other social media tools, legal professionals (and others) should be wary of default settings. The good news is that LinkedIn offers a large number of choices for personalizing your experience, choosing appropriate settings, and revealing and managing your information in the way that makes the most sense for you. LinkedIn also assembles the controls in one convenient location.

Work your way through all the settings step by step, either when you create your account or the next time you log in to your account. It will take only a few minutes. Then plan to revisit your settings once or twice a year, if you learn that LinkedIn has made changes, or if you notice that you are receiving too many e-mails or have other annoyances. Often what might be bothering you about LinkedIn can be remedied with a quick change to your settings. Most of the most vocal complaints we have heard from LinkedIn users have involved issues that could easily be addressed by simple settings changes.

IMPORTANT NOTE: LinkedIn has historically made changes to the types of settings available, where users go to manage the settings, and the ways that settings are displayed and organized. The good news is that these changes have been positive ones, especially in the way LinkedIn has collected and organized the settings. The bad news is that there's a good chance that the description of the current setting options we describe in this chapter might not match what you see on LinkedIn when you actually read this chapter. If that's the case, simply treat this chapter as a checklist of what settings are likely to be available and as encouragement to explore the available settings on your own.

You can also check the section on managing account settings in the LinkedIn Help Center ***https://www.linkedin.com/help/linkedin/answer/66***.

To get started, simply hover over your thumbnail picture (the Me tab) on the right-hand side of the top navigation bar until the dropdown menu appears. Then click on the Privacy & Settings item.

You will be taken to a handy location where LinkedIn gives you many ways to tailor your privacy controls, settings for Profiles, communications, Groups, Companies, applications, and other account options. The current major groupings are: Account, Privacy, Ads, and Communication.

Account Settings

Login and security

- ► Add or remove email addresses on your account
- ► Add a phone number in case you have trouble signing in
- ► Change password

Where you're signed in—see your active sessions, and sign out if you'd like

Two-step verification [Two-step verification is an important new trend in security and helps prevent someone from getting into and taking over your account. Two-step verification involves "something you know" (your password) and "something you have" (your cell phone). If you turn this option on (and we definitely recommend that you do), you will provide LinkedIn your cell phone number and receive a text with a code that you will need to enter whenever you access your LinkedIn account from a new device. This approach provides an additional level of protection in exchange for a relatively minor inconvenience.]

Site preferences

► Language

► Autoplay videos

► Showing profile photos

► Feed preferences

► Name, location, and industry—how your name and other profile fields

Subscriptions and payments

► Manage Premium account

► View purchase history

► View Microsoft accounts you've connected to your LinkedIn account

► View services you've authorized and manage data sharing

► Manage your Twitter info and activity on your LinkedIn account

Account management

► Merging LinkedIn accounts

► Closing your LinkedIn account

Privacy

How others see your profile and network information

► Choose how your profile appears to non-logged in members via search engines or permitted services

► Who can see your email address

► Who can see your connections

► Viewers of this profile also viewed

► Who can see your last name

► Choose how you want your name to appear

► Representing your organization and interests

► Profile visibility off

► Choose whether work experience descriptions from your LinkedIn profile can be shown in Resume Assistant, a feature within Microsoft Word.

How others see your LinkedIn activity

► Profile viewing options—choose whether you're visible or viewing in private mode

► Who can see when you are on LinkedIn

► Share job changes, education changes, and work anniversaries

- ▶ Notifying connections when you're in the news

- ▶ Mentions or tags by others

- ▶ Choose whether other members can mention or tag you

How LinkedIn uses your data

- ▶ Review the data that you've provided, and make changes if you'd like

- ▶ Download an archive of your account data, posts, connections, and more

- ▶ Manage who can discover your profile from your email address

- ▶ Choose who can discover your profile if they are not connected to you but have your email address

- ▶ Manage who can discover your profile from your phone number

- ▶ Manage or sync contacts to connect with people you know directly from your address book

- ▶ Manage or sync calendar to get timely updates about who you'll be meeting with

- ▶ Salary data on LinkedIn

- ▶ See and delete your salary data

- ▶ Clear all previous searches performed on LinkedIn

- ▶ Choose what details you provide about your personal demographics

- ▶ Choose whether your data can be made available to trusted services for policy and academic research

Job seeking preferences

► Choose what information LinkedIn saves when you submit a job application.

► Let recruiters know you're open to opportunities

► Signal your interest to recruiters at companies you have created job alerts for

► Sharing your profile when you click apply

► Stored job applicant accounts

Blocking and hiding

► Choose who can follow you and see your public updates

► Blocking—see your list, and make changes if you'd like

► See who you have unfollowed, and resume following if you'd like

Communications

Channels

► Manage the alerts you receive in the Notifications tab

► Email frequency—choose what types of emails you wish to receive

► SMS frequency

Preferences

► Who can send you invitations

► Choose who can send you invitations to connect

- ► Messages from members and partners
- ► Read receipts and typing indicators
- ► Messaging reply suggestions
- ► Group invitations—choose whether you want to receive invitations to join groups

LinkedIn messages

Participate in research

Ads

General advertising preferences

- ► Insights on websites you visited
- ► Ads beyond LinkedIn
- ► Profile data for ad personalization

Data collected on LinkedIn (see more relevant ads)

- ► Interest categories
- ► Connections
- ► Location
- ► Demographics
- ► Companies you follow
- ► Groups
- ► Education
- ► Job information
- ► Employer

Third party data

► Interactions with businesses

► Ad-related actions

Another place to change some important settings is on the Profile page that you (not others) see when you are logged in to LinkedIn. Clicking on the phrase "Edit public profile & URL" opens a page with some important Profile settings all located in one place.

You can edit the URL LinkedIn assigns to your profile and create a custom URL. For example, Allison's profile has a URL of ***https:// www.linkedin.com/in/allisoncshieldslegalease/***. You can also easily dial up and down the settings of who can see what on your Profile. While you are visiting those settings, be sure to take advantage of the LinkedIn badge creator to generate a LinkedIn graphic with a link that you can use in email signatures, your blog, or elsewhere.

Settings Recommendations

We generally recommend taking the grand tour of all the settings once a year to confirm that they are set the way that you want and still make sense, to see what new setting options LinkedIn has added, and to do some general upkeep and maintenance, such as changing your password, especially if your LinkedIn password is the same as what you are using on anywhere else or is not a strong password. If someone hacks your LinkedIn account, the hacker can damage your professional presence in view of your most important contacts.

That said, here are a few recommendations for you to consider:

► Add a secondary email address and a phone number to your account, especially if you have set up your account with a work email or work phone number.

- ► Turn on two-step verification (also known as multi-factor authentication).

- ► Stop complaining about how much email you get from LinkedIn and turn off email alerts or adjust email notifications to something that works for you. Just a few good selections in this area can reduce or even eliminate annoyances you might have with LinkedIn e-mail notifications.

- ► If your Profile settings are as private as possible, you are absolutely limiting who can see your Profile, and that includes contacts and potential employers. If your purpose for creating a LinkedIn account and Profile is for purposes of networking, business development, marketing, job seeking, reputation building, etc., making it private or hiding information works against you. Compare this to networking in real life—would you go to a networking event or look for a job and not tell anyone who you are, what you're looking for, or what your experience is? And hide in a corner and not wear a name badge? You have to be visible for people to find you. More than likely, you will be better off limiting the viewing of certain data elements (e.g., phone number) rather than limiting who can view your whole Profile.

To learn even more about how you can protect yourself on LinkedIn, visit the Safety Center at ***https://safety.linkedin.com/***.

4

DEVELOPING YOUR LINKEDIN STRATEGY

A s the lottery people like to say, you can't win if you don't play. There is a definite correlation between usage, especially quality of usage, and the value you get from LinkedIn. We can't even count the times legal professionals have told us that they are "on LinkedIn," but don't fully understand what it does or why it might benefit them. Those comments are what motivated us to write this book in the first place.

We sometimes say that LinkedIn is simultaneously the most used and most underused social media platform for the legal industry. When we ask questions about how people use LinkedIn, we find that their approaches tend to be very passive and they simply aren't familiar the main features of LinkedIn. In the next chapter, we talk about the three building blocks of LinkedIn—Profiles, Connection and Participation. Often, light LinkedIn users are completely unaware of one or two of those three key building blocks.

In fact, when we speak about LinkedIn, we can almost see the light bulbs switching on as people start to understand how LinkedIn really works and the ways it can supplement and enhance real world networking efforts. In simplest terms, LinkedIn attempts to map the professional connections and relationships you have in the real world to the Internet. It also gives you ways to map your online social network back into the real world.

LinkedIn provides powerful tools to connect to your network, and, this is the key insight, to *participate in your networks for the benefit of yourself and others in your network*. Once people understand what LinkedIn does, they seem to see the ways they can use it to increase the value their use of LinkedIn and their professional and business relationships. Over the years, we have often had legal professionals tell us after hearing us talk about LinkedIn that they realized that they had missed the point of LinkedIn and planned to start to use it better.

What is a LinkedIn Strategy?

To get the most out of LinkedIn, you need to have a strategy. That strategy needs to be reviewed from time to time and adjusted to meet your needs and the needs of your evolving LinkedIn and real-world networks.

Think of LinkedIn like you would any other "real life" networking group: to get the most out of it, you need to participate. If you just set up a bare bones LinkedIn profile and passively sit back and wait for invitations to connect to arrive in your Inbox, or invite connections without giving any thought to why they would want to connect with you or how you can help them, you're just like the lawyer who attends networking events and hands out business cards, but does not follow up. In either case, current business and future relationships are unlikely to follow. LinkedIn is not a magic wand.

Networking is about building and fostering relationships. Relationships, whether online or in the real world, need to be nurtured. To gain the most benefit possible from LinkedIn, you need to be actively engaged. Simple efforts like sending personalized invitations to connect, following up with your connections, making an effort to help others, and providing value to your network can make a world of difference.

Before jumping into specific activities on LinkedIn, you should think about how you network in the real world, who your target audience is, and what type of participation makes sense for you personally and professionally. How do you network to get referrals and new clients? How do you reach out to existing clients? Do you write articles, speak, participate on boards or community groups, play golf or volunteer for a local charity? Once you understand that, the ways that you might use LinkedIn will start to take shape.

There are also some basic philosophical questions that you will want to answer. Do you want your LinkedIn Connections to be only people who have met in person? Will you emphasize quality of Connections over quantity of Connections? (There are benefits to both approaches.) How willing are you to take chances in accepting unsolicited invitations or sending invitations to people outside your comfort zone, especially authors and experts in your field? We have some opinions about these questions, as you will see throughout this book, but your answers should be individual to you.

With the answers to those questions in mind, we have four other questions to help you develop your LinkedIn strategy (or strategies).

- ► What are you "hiring" LinkedIn to do for you?
- ► How do you make yourself "discoverable" within your network?
- ► How do you bring the real world into LinkedIn and LinkedIn into the real world?
- ► How do you want to communicate with your network?

What are you "hiring" LinkedIn to do for you?

We are big fans of the jobs-to-be-done approach associated with Clayton Christensen and others. We summarized it in the Introduction. We have included a number of jobs-to-be-done resources in the Resources section of this book. Here, we want to focus on the "what are you hiring X to do for you?" aspect of the approach.

In this case, the question becomes, "What are you hiring LinkedIn to do for you?" The more specific and detailed your answer to that question becomes, the better your LinkedIn strategy will be. That concept is simple, but the execution can be surprisingly difficult.

A tool we have found to be useful is Alex Osterwalder's Value Proposition Canvas (**https://www.strategyzer.com/canvas/value-proposition-canvas**). This tool helps you create a map of your thinking and approach, and then see how closely your action maps to the results that you want to achieve.

First, spell out the job to be done or problem to solve. Then list the pains you hope to overcome and the gains you would like to achieve.

Next, describe what you intend to use LinkedIn for in connection with that job to be done. For example, if you need a new job, your first instinct might be to say that you will "use LinkedIn to get a new job" by using LinkedIn in a certain way. You then list the pains that using LinkedIn in that way will alleviate and the gains that it will help you achieve.

The third step is stepping back and seeing how well the pains and gains sections match. On the first attempt, the answer usually will be "not so well." That's the information you want. You will then refine your approach and run it through the value proposition canvas again until you find a good fit and understand what it is that you want.

Examples always help. Imagine you are an estate planning lawyer and you want to get new clients. Your initial job to be done might be to get new clients. Your initial thinking might be to try to connect to as many high-net-worth potential clients as you can by sending them invitations to connect on LinkedIn. Even without doing this exercise, we can assure you that the match between pains and gains will be poor.

After a couple of attempts, you might refine your job to be done to increase the number of high-quality referrals from your network and your use of LinkedIn to be creating, growing and nurturing a network of tax accountants, financial planners, life insurance agents, assisted living operators, trust officers, bankers, nursing home owners, and the like. Your strategy might include sending out news and links that provide value to people in that referral network. The job to be done subtly has changed from getting new business to getting more referral clients. That's something that LinkedIn can definitely help you with.

Similarly, "finding a new job" might not be the best job to be done. "Helping me connect with people who can help me get interviews" is a slightly different job, but one that can help you create a much more effective LinkedIn strategy.

Other ideas? When Dennis moved from St. Louis to Ann Arbor, his LinkedIn strategy changed for a period of time to focus on using his existing LinkedIn network to help build out and extend his Michigan network on LinkedIn by focusing on second-degree LinkedIn connections. LinkedIn can also help you obtain competitive intelligence about other legal professionals, firms, or your clients' competitors. Regularly check LinkedIn for information about industries, clients, and potential clients. You can join groups, monitor Company Pages, or watch for job openings, new hires, and departures to bring you relevant competitive intelligence on a regular basis.

Often, we find that people see LinkedIn as a one-size-fits-all service and do not tailor it to what might help them. This is one of the most common reasons people don't believe that they are getting value out of LinkedIn. And it is easy to fix. Try some experiments.

How do you make yourself "discoverable" within your network?

Many legal professionals have a "Field of Dreams" approach to marketing. If they do good work, magically clients will come to them. To them, law is a profession and "business" is a dirty word. Marketing and sales are even worse.

When people want to hire you for a job or a project, they need to be able to find you when they are looking. Millions of people use LinkedIn as one of the ways they find people. If you search your name in Google (and you should), you are very likely to find that your LinkedIn Profile is either the first search result or one of the first few. People are more likely to head to your LinkedIn Profile than going to your law firm bio, especially if your Profile ranks higher in the search results.

An underappreciated aspect of LinkedIn is how discoverable it makes you. People look to your headline, your shared connections with them, alumni connections, articles, presentations, and much more. Those things establish what is called "social map" of your network and show people how you and your network compares and interacts with their own. They surface the commonalities that people rely on to make decisions about who they want to work with.

A simple first step is simply to imagine that you are someone looking for you on LinkedIn and try to find yourself and learn about you and what you do. What is that experience like? What do you learn about yourself? Is it want you want others to learn about you? Even better, ask a trusted friend, family member, or colleague to do the same experiment and be candid with you about their observations.

For the next step, think about someone who you consider a competitor. Try to find them on LinkedIn. What do you learn? Can you change your strategy on LinkedIn to improve your discoverability by tweaking your headline, connecting to fellow alumni, joining groups, or other easy efforts that will improve your discoverability? Spoiler alert: yes, you can.

How do you bring the real world into LinkedIn and LinkedIn into the real world?

LinkedIn is an extension of real-life networking, so you should be connecting with people from all kinds of industries and professions on LinkedIn, just as you would in real life. Those connections can be potential clients or referral sources. Many of them may be legal professionals, who could also be referral sources, whether they are legal professionals who practice in different areas of the law or in different jurisdictions, but we would recommend that you expand your network beyond just legal professionals to make a richer network.

For example, an estate planning lawyer might want their LinkedIn audience to include tax accountants, financial planners, life insurance agents, trust officers, bankers, nursing home owners and many others. If your posts are helpful to those groups, you might get much more benefit out of LinkedIn than if you think only of legal professionals as your target. You can also coordinate and amplify your content from elsewhere on LinkedIn. For example, if you're already posting on other social networks, it's easy to post the same content, links, etc. on LinkedIn at the same time, either cutting and pasting or using tools like Buffer, HootSuite and others that will allow you to post on multiple networks at the same time. This multi-faceted approach will help you expand your audience by activating several platforms.

Many people see use of LinkedIn as only an Internet activity. However, LinkedIn becomes especially valuable when you use it to supplement or complement real world activities, even in the simplest ways. Traveling? Search LinkedIn to find connections to visit or meet with while in their cities. Meeting someone for lunch? Connect on LinkedIn and view their photo so that you recognize them when you meet at the restaurant. Take what you learn in LinkedIn to send congratulatory notes, call people on their birthdays, or find people in common to talk about in person. Use LinkedIn to follow up with new connections to strengthen new relationships or to reconnect with former colleagues or classmates you may have lost touch with.

It often takes 7-9 "touches" before someone will do business with you. Why not accelerate your offline relationships by connecting online, too? LinkedIn makes it easy for you to stay in touch and find out what clients, colleagues and strategic partners in the real world are doing, and to discover commonalities or challenges that might lead to additional business. Think of LinkedIn as a supplement to real world relationships and not an entirely separate area.

How do you want to communicate with your network?

Another important strategic question is the interrelated issue of how best to communicate through LinkedIn.

In the real world, you might send people birthday cards, holiday cards, copies of articles, congratulatory and thank you notes, and much more. All of those things map to LinkedIn and are easier to do and do for more people on a more regular basis than you might do by hand.

Here's a simple example. If you like to mail (or email) clients copies of your articles or other information that might be useful or of interest to them, you can, in a few minutes, send a Post on LinkedIn with a description of the article, a key point or highlighted quote, and the hyperlink to the article. You are simultaneously sending it to your whole network. Using the simple technique of "tagging" people (discussed in Chapter 17), you can alert specific people that you have sent the Post and mentioned them.

Our belief is that if you map what you do best in the real world to LinkedIn, you will have the best success. If you are a birthday card person, wish people happy birthday on LinkedIn. If you send people congratulatory notes, it is easy to send congratulations on LinkedIn. LinkedIn essentially makes it a one-click communication.

The LinkedIn Feedback Loop

You can take your LinkedIn game to the next level by experimenting with communications and other LinkedIn features and using them as a feedback loop. A number of LinkedIn features can be used creatively to test and give you feedback on the success of your LinkedIn efforts.

After you submit a Post, you will be able to see information on views, likes, and comments. This data will let you judge the effectiveness of topics or approaches, and even whether there are better days or times to send Posts. Looking at the "likes" will help you see who is in your audience and "likes" from second-degree connections will reveal likely candidates for you to send invitations to make a first-degree connection. You will have the opportunity to reply to the comments of others and expand your thoughts. The key feedback, however, will be to test what topics hit home with your network. (You can see more on LinkedIn analytics and what to do with them in Chapter 18)

Both Allison and Dennis tweak their Headlines from time to time to reflect services that they are offering, new roles, and whether certain words appeal more to their audiences. For example, is it better to say, "partner in X law firm" or "Michigan fintech lawyer"? How about "advisor" vs. "consultant"? You can do some experimenting to see if there is any difference in the level of engagement or results you see. (For more on your LinkedIn Headline, see Chapter 6)

The Skills and Endorsements section of your Profile can reveal a lot about how people think about you and what you do. If you find that people are adding votes for you as a litigator and for your legal research skills, you might realize that you need to clarify to your network that what you focus on is appellate advocacy for patent infringement cases. Using that feedback from LinkedIn can help you hone your message and educate your network (and choose different Skills to show as the Featured Skills on your Profile). Similarly, you might experiment with your Headline or About section if you are looking to highlight or focus on a practice area.

Strategy is More Important than You Might Think

Our best advice is to keep asking "What Job Are You Hiring LinkedIn to Do?" Most people automatically see the value of LinkedIn when they are searching for a job. But when they aren't looking for a job, people may lose clarity about the purpose of using LinkedIn. Many legal professionals have been told that LinkedIn is an essential new tool for getting new clients. That is far different than searching for a job, and might not even be a good use of LinkedIn for you.

Many legal professionals, rightfully, simply do not see how LinkedIn can be used to reach potential clients and convert them to actual clients. That's OK—you can hire LinkedIn for many different jobs. For example, you might hire LinkedIn chiefly as a publisher for content that you create that doesn't have another home, as a platform to showcase your expertise and build your reputation, and/or as a way for journalist and other media to find you.

We often stress that the great value of LinkedIn for most legal professionals will come from **_creating and sustaining your referral networks_**. If that is the job you hire LinkedIn to do, your use of LinkedIn will probably make more sense to you than it does now, and you will have better ideas of what you can do on LinkedIn.

Moving to the next level on LinkedIn requires a thoughtful strategy that evolves over time. Your strategy will likely change as your situation and your roles change.

As a final thought, there may be no better resource than LinkedIn to help you reconnect with people who were important in your career but with whom you have lost contact. Make that part of your overall strategy.

5

THE THREE BUILDING BLOCKS OF LINKEDIN: PROFILE, CONNECTIONS AND PARTICIPATION

O ur biggest insight from writing our first LinkedIn book was the simple, three-part framework we found for understanding LinkedIn. We've gotten a lot of great feedback on that framework and many people inside and outside the legal industry use the three-part approach or something very similar to it.

As we mentioned in the Introduction, the three essential building blocks of LinkedIn are:

► Profiles (who you are),

► Connections (who you know) and

► Participation (how you interact with connections).

Even if you think you have "done everything" with LinkedIn or "given up" on it, focusing on each of these elements separately will help you analyze your efforts and give you additional ideas for improving your presence, your experience and your results. Often, people need the most work on Participation, but we are surprised at how many people who think that they are advanced LinkedIn users have out-of-date Profiles or have not adopted a systematic approach to adding Connections. The three essential building blocks gives you a simple and effective way to analyze and improve your use of LinkedIn.

It's a simple concept. The next three sections of this book will walk you through each of the three building blocks in detail and offer you many practical ways to level up your use of LinkedIn.

PART II

PROFILE

6

YOUR BASIC PROFILE

Your Profile is truly the foundation of your LinkedIn presence. LinkedIn users will go to your Profile to find out information about you, and it is where much of your LinkedIn content resides or is accessed from. You can also think of your Profile as an online resume or biography, complete with multimedia elements, examples of your work, and recommendations or references. We consider it to be the first of the three essential LinkedIn building blocks.

Getting Started Building Your Profile

When you set up your account, LinkedIn will automatically get you started on your professional Profile. The first few screens you encounter after you set up your account will walk you through filling in blanks to provide information about your current and former employment, your education and more, and those answers are automatically transferred to your Profile. But completing these forms is just the first step in creating a complete Profile.

As you scroll down your Profile, under your "About" section (which used to be called the Summary, and as of the date of publication of this book, is still labeled Summary in LinkedIn's prompts to improve your Profile), you will see your Dashboard, where LinkedIn provides a snapshot of information for you. At the top of the Dashboard, you will see a designation that indicates to LinkedIn how complete your Profile is, with the highest level being "All Star." You'll also be able to see how many people viewed your Profile, how many viewed your Posts, and how often you appeared in Search. These are all indications of how strong—and how effective—your Profile is.

LinkedIn provides some guides to help you complete or add to your Profile. For example, until you have reached "All Star" status, LinkedIn will provide you with suggestions about how to improve your Profile at the top of your Home screen and your Profile and through the Profile Strength Meter in your Dashboard. Even after you have reached "All Star" status, you will see the blue "Add profile section" box in your introduction card when you view your Profile. As you scroll down when viewing your Profile, this blue box will remain at the top of the page, so you can add sections whenever you wish. We will discuss adding sections to your Profile more in the next chapter.

Aligning your LinkedIn Profile with your Strategy and Goals

If you have taken the time to think about your LinkedIn strategy and goals as we discussed in Chapter 4, now is the time to start putting that strategy into action. As you are writing your Profile, you will want to keep in mind the job you're hiring LinkedIn to do for you. Consider the audience you are trying to reach, the ideas, information and services that are important to them, and how you can add value through your LinkedIn Profile.

What does your audience need to know about what you do and who you do it for? What words are they likely to search to find someone like you? How do they express the problem—or the symptoms of the problem—that you solve for them? These are all questions to keep in mind as you create or refine your LinkedIn Profile. Always keep in mind the perspective and needs of the desired audience for your Profile.

Editing Your Profile

To fully complete or edit your Profile, navigate to your Profile. The easiest way to do so is to click on your name or photo in the left sidebar from your Home page on LinkedIn (the page you first encounter when you log into your account), or by clicking the "Me" tab and then choosing "View Profile" "On the mobile app, click on your photo at the top left, then click on "View Profile."

You will see small icons that look like a pencil in various places on your Profile. Clicking on the pencil icon will bring up a pop-up box to allow you to edit each of the items within that section of your Profile.

Let's walk through the key sections of your Profile and what to think about when editing each of those key sections.

Your Introduction Card

LinkedIn calls the first section of your Profile your "Introduction Card." This section contains your name, your Profile Photo, Headline, and About section/Summary, and also pulls some information from the rest of your Profile to display, such as your present place of employment, number of Connections, and so on.

Profile Photo

Your photograph is an important part of your Profile. Professional photographs are preferable, but do not wait until you have time to have a professional photograph taken. It is perfectly acceptable to use a high-quality digital image from your own camera or a cropped family or personal photograph of your face—as long as it looks professional and presents you well. Crop the photo so that it shows your head and shoulders only to get maximum exposure for your face, but take a critical look at the photo once it has been cropped—sometimes cropping a photo can make an otherwise professional-looking photo look odd or inappropriate. In addition, many interactions on LinkedIn use thumbnail photos which can make it difficult to tell who is in the photo if it isn't cropped correctly.

LinkedIn is a business network, not a social network, so no selfies, party photos, vacation photos, or photos with pets, please! We also recommend that you avoid any photo that includes someone other than yourself. As we discuss in Chapter 22 on personal branding, the brand is You. You may like the photo of you in front of your office window or your library of (obsolete) law books, but you're much better off with a plain background for your LinkedIn Profile photo.

Most disturbing are the lawyer Profiles with no photo at all. Humans relate to human faces, and many people remember faces much more easily than they remember names. Your photo is important for purposes of recognition, but also to ensure that you don't miss out on connections. A notable exception might be if you were having issues with a "stalker" or had other safety concerns.

Take a look at the photos used by people you know and admire on LinkedIn to get an idea of what type of photo you should use. Consider using the same photograph on your LinkedIn profile that you use across other online platforms so that people recognize you as the same person. It is a good idea to keep this photo current—regardless of whether you like the photo from 20 years ago better. And if you change your hairstyle significantly, grow or shave a beard, get new glasses or otherwise update your appearance, be sure to update your LinkedIn photo as well.

Why is your photograph important?

- ► Using the default icon in place of an actual photo makes it look like your account is inactive or you don't pay any attention to it, which makes other users more reluctant to engage or connect with you.

- ► A lot of us (especially as we get older!) may recognize faces even if they don't remember names, so your photo can be a powerful reminder of who you are.

- ► Many people use LinkedIn to prepare for a meeting; having a photograph on LinkedIn makes you easier to recognize and helps establish a connection when you meet someone in person.

- ► People do business with those whom they know, like, and trust; posting a photograph helps your audience feel that they "know" you even if they haven't met you.

Click on the pencil icon in your Introduction Card, then on the pencil icon next to the headshot icon and follow the instructions to upload a photograph from your computer. If you change your mind or get a better picture, you can upload a new photograph in place of your old one. Updating you photo should take you only a minute or two. We give you permission to change your photo as often as you like, as long as the new photo helps you get the job that you are hiring LinkedIn done.

Your Profile photo can be almost any size over 400 x 400 pixels. Obviously, sharp, higher resolution photos are best.

Profile Link

If you search on your own name in Google, you'll probably see how high your public LinkedIn Profile ranks in the results. As a result, you might be surprised by how many people find you first through your LinkedIn Profile. The default URL for your LinkedIn Profile contains a long set of gibberish characters. It is just below your photo and looks something like this: ***http://www.linkedin.com/in/mary-smith/26/4a1/114***.

You can change the URL to eliminate the nonsense characters and substitute your name, your firm's name or other branding you use to make it easier to find, advertise, and share your LinkedIn Profile. Get rid of the random numbers and letters to customize the link to include just your name and a keyword or two, or your name and firm name. Currently, all you need to do is find the link for "Edit public profile & URL" in the right column on your Profile page and make the change you want, assuming no one else has already taken it. It's a simple way to make it easier to find your Profile, show that you are LinkedIn savvy, and reinforce your "brand."

You can find the Public Profile link in your contact information in your Introduction Card. Alternatively, you can get there directly by going to your Settings (see Chapter 3), choosing Settings and Privacy, and editing your Public Profile URL from there. Sometimes LinkedIn gives you a link to edit your Public Profile information on the top right of your Home page as well.

Other Links

LinkedIn allows three links in the contact information portion of the Introduction Card. You can link to your website, blog, firm bio, and so forth. Use all three opportunities if you can, even if you don't have your own online presence outside of LinkedIn. For example, you could link to your bio on your firm's website, your firm's Home page, and the practice area page on your firm's site as your three links.

We strongly recommend that you do not use LinkedIn's default settings for the link titles (e.g., "Company"). Instead, customize the link titles by clicking on the edit (pencil) icon under contact info, and then choosing "other" from the dropdown box next to the link's URL. Then you can fill in your own name for the link. Use keywords or the actual name of the page or site you are linking to.

Your Professional Headline

Your Headline is a one-line description that often accompanies your name when you interact on LinkedIn. Your Headline is the line that appears under your name on LinkedIn. When users first encounter you on LinkedIn, they may not be looking at your Profile; they may see you as a suggestion in People You May Know on their Network page, in search results, in a list of connections, or in a LinkedIn Group. In many of those cases, all they will see is your photo, name, and your Professional Headline.

The professional headline field defaults to your current position if you do not create a separate Headline, and when you change your current position, LinkedIn gives you the option to automatically change your Headline as well. You can make your Headline much more descriptive and useful than just your current position or title (such as associate or partner).

We recommend that you use all of the 120 characters allotted in the Headline field and provide information helpful to someone outside your firm. Describe your practice area, your clients, or your services and make sure you use "lawyer" or "attorney" in your description for those all-important search results. Otherwise, LinkedIn users can't distinguish you from a retail sales "associate" or a partner in any other kind of business, such as an accounting firm.

Think of your Headline as your LinkedIn elevator speech or your virtual introduction. It should be short and to the point, but it should communicate enough information about you to entice people to want to know more. In the case of LinkedIn, you want your Headline to convince users to click on your name and view your full Profile or to connect with you.

Know your audience. Think about what is most important to your audience or the people you want to connect with on LinkedIn. Your Professional Headline is a valuable tool that can communicate your area of practice, your knowledge and experience and to distinguish yourself from other legal professionals. It should be a differentiator that helps you to stand out in search results and it should be descriptive so that when people see your Professional Headline, they immediately know what you do.

Be descriptive. Don't make the common mistake made by many legal professionals of limiting your Headline to just your title (Associate, Partner, etc.). Include your practice areas or the types of work you do for clients. Use keywords that your audience might use to search for a legal professional in your practice area. Consider including the name of your firm as well—it won't always be obvious to LinkedIn users if they're not looking at your full Profile when they encounter your name.

But don't stop there. Even your title and firm name ("Partner at Stark and Snow, P.C") are not enough. If a user is not familiar with your firm, this information may not be enough even to communicate that you are a lawyer (Stark and Snow could be an accounting firm, for example). Note that if you are considering leaving your firm, you might want to start using a Headline that does not include the firm name.

Compare these Headline examples:

- ► Partner **OR** Partner at Grantham and Carson, LLP, Management-side Labor and Employment Law Trial Attorney

- ► Associate at Pearson & Pearson, P.C **OR** Elder Law and Estate Planning Attorney at The Stolar Partnership

- ► Trial Partner at Florrick & Agos **OR** Partner, Scott &,Schrute, Risk Management and Legal Malpractice Attorney

- ► Data privacy lawyer **OR** Data breach incident response, remediation, and litigation defense for healthcare providers

- ► Senior Managing Counsel at ABC University **OR** Leader of Technology Transfer Legal Team at ABC University

If these headlines appeared in search results, which one in each pair would you be more likely to select?

Revising your Headline

Certain key events (getting a job, losing a job, promotions, etc.) will trigger the need to revise your Headline (along with the rest of your Profile). There's no hard and fast rule, and much depends on your purpose and audience, and how fast those things change. You also might consider revising your Headline based on what is happening with your practice or in the marketplace, to add new phrasing or incorporate new terms you notice your clients are using.

Revise your Headline as often as you need to. But keep in mind that when you revise your Headline, LinkedIn may send your connections a notification that you have a new job. If that isn't the case and you're just tweaking your Headline, you may want to turn off those notifications before you make your Headline changes.

The Benefit-driven Headline

Legal professionals who want to really stand out on LinkedIn might want to consider writing a benefit-driven Headline.

What is a benefit-driven Headline? It is a Headline that focuses on the benefits that you offer to your clients, rather than your title or what you do.

For example, instead of, "Elder Law and Estate Planning Associate Attorney at Stark & Snow," you might want to focus your Headline on the benefits that you provide to your clients, saying something like, "Helping families protect their aging loved ones and their legacy." You might even try creatively combining these, using all the available 120 characters.

The Professional Headline is one of the most important elements of your LinkedIn Profile. It probably will be the main description anyone who sees you on LinkedIn if you like, comment, or appear on someone's "who you may know" list. Take some time today to sit down and think about how you can be more creative with your Headline to attract clients, referral sources, hiring partners, or even the media.

About

Next is your **About** section, which in some places is called the Summary. At the time this book was published, we observed that LinkedIn appears to be transitioning between "Summary" and "About." You might see some differences depending where and when you are looking at this feature.

You can edit this section by clicking on the pencil icon in the separate "About" card on the desktop version or in the mobile app. This section permits approximately 330 words (or approximately

2000 characters) of description. Because the Summary/About section often is read more than the description under the listing for your current position, do not overlook it. As a practical matter, if someone is intrigued by your Headline, their next stop will be your About section. If the About section is missing or perfunctory, they might not even go on to read the descriptions under your job listings further down in your Profile.

This section is an opportunity to expand on what you've begun with your Headline, to describe what you do and who you do it for in more detail, and expand on your "elevator pitch." It is a place for you to summarize all of your experience. If you consider LinkedIn as a professional resume of sorts then the Summary section is the cover letter to that resume—it's an opportunity for you to tie together all of your experience, volunteer work and education and explain how they inform what you do today and how you serve your clients and customers. It is a mini biography.

We suggest that you write the About section in the first person; when you network in person, you speak in the first person, and doing so on LinkedIn makes you more approachable. Resist the urge to copy-and-paste your bio from your firm's website without changing it.

At its most basic, a good LinkedIn About section addresses:

- ► Who you are
- ► How you got where you are
- ► What you do now, for whom and why
- ► Where you are going/what you anticipate for the future (particularly with reference to your clients)

Essentially, your About section is a snapshot of you and your practice in about 2000 characters. It is an opportunity for you to define who you are and what you do in a global way—not compartmentalized into sections or individual positions, like the rest of your

Profile. Take a look at the ways people you admire have written their About sections to get some good ideas.

You'll want to put the most important information in your About section at the beginning—this is because LinkedIn does not display the entire section default. Instead, only a portion (approximately 200 or so characters on desktop and 20-25 words on mobile) will appear unless the visitor to your Profile clicks on the "Show more" link to see your complete About section. As a result, the introduction to your About section must written with that in mind. Your goal in the first sentence is to get people to click on the "Show more" link, so make it as compelling as possible.

Although your LinkedIn profile is *about* you, it is not written *for* you—it is written for the people you want to read it (or even better, to contact you after they read it). And that means it has to address what is important to *them* – what they most want to know. This isn't necessarily the same as what you think they should want to know.

Your About section should also include some form of the following:

▶ Identification of your target audience

▶ A discussion of that audience's most common problems or challenges

▶ Your solution (how you help clients or solve that problem for them)

▶ How your solution is different

The About section can also be a good place to add items that are important for lawyers to include on their Profiles, but that do not have any other obvious home on LinkedIn, such as jurisdictions where you are admitted to practice and disclaimers required by your jurisdiction (see Chapter 28 for more about required disclaimers on LinkedIn).

Although only the first portion of your About section initially appears to LinkedIn users, when users who are *not* logged on to LinkedIn click on your Profile, they will see what LinkedIn calls your public profile. If you choose to display the About section on your public profile, viewers will see the entire section without any extra clicks required. (Although the public profile does not show any media you've added to your Profile.)

Take advantage of the space LinkedIn provides for you in this section to give LinkedIn users and potential connections a snapshot of your professional expertise.

Specialties is a shorter section at the end of the About section (256 total characters) that you might remember, but that has now been phased out. If you have been on LinkedIn for a while and had this section filled in, it will continue to appear at the end of your Summary unless you voluntarily remove it. Since it may present an ethical problem due to many jurisdictions' prohibitions against lawyers identifying themselves as "specialists" in a particular field, you may want to remove it and just incorporate those keywords or practice areas into your Summary. (We talk about the "specialties" issue further in the ethics discussion later in this book.)

Experience/Positions

Below the About section you will find the Experience section of your Profile. The Experience section displays your positions in reverse chronological order.

We recommend that you list all of your relevant past and present experience and positions, including the name of the company or firm for which you worked, the dates you worked there, your title, and a description of what you did. Adding all of your previous positions will improve your "discoverability" on LinkedIn and help you find former colleagues with whom to connect. For older jobs, you might create a "catch-all" listing to address what could be seen as gaps in your resume and bundle summary descriptions of those jobs all in one place.

As with your Headline and About sections, choose keywords that are meaningful to and recognizable by your target audience. Include important experiences or skills that help differentiate you from other legal professionals in your field. You have 1000 characters to describe each position. We will discuss in Chapter 11 how LinkedIn uses this information to help you connect to current and former colleagues.

LinkedIn does not allow you to change the order of the position listings within the Experience section unless you have two or more "current" positions—in that case, you can choose the order that the current positions are displayed on your Profile. This feature can be important when you want to include a "side hustle" or volunteer positions as current positions, but you want your main job to show up first on the list.

You may list bar association or other community positions (e.g., board service) under Experience, too. Listing these activities helps others find you when they search for the organization name and makes it easier to invite others associated with that organization to connect. If you don't want to list these positions under Experience, you may choose to list these positions under "Groups and Associations" in the Additional Information section or in the optional Organizations or Volunteering & Causes sections. (See Chapter 7 for more information on these additional Profile sections).

Education

After Experience, the next section that appears on your LinkedIn Profile is Education. School alumni can be valuable contacts, as we will discuss in Chapter 11. Include your educational information for law school and for any undergraduate or other postsecondary education.

It might also be useful, especially for young people or those who attended private high schools or even elementary schools, to add these to your list for enhanced "discoverability" and to help make other alumni connections. Do not forget to add awards, volunteer groups, affiliations, study abroad and the like. All of these can help you establish real world connections through commonalities. Belonging to the same sorority or fraternity as someone else is an obvious example where knowledge of that commonality can open doors.

Skills and Endorsements

Below Education on your Profile is the Skills and Endorsements section. Thinking about "skills" may be a bit foreign for legal professionals, but as you will see in Chapter 16, LinkedIn returns search results directly linked to the Skills section in your Profile, and you need at least five skills listed on your Profile for LinkedIn to consider it complete. In addition, this section has become even more visible since the addition of Endorsements, which we will discuss further in Chapter 16. All in all, if there are no ethical obstacles in your jurisdiction, it is important to add something to Skills for the best search results possible.

Skills can include not only your practice areas but also the skills you use within those practice areas, such as negotiating contracts or trial advocacy. Be specific with your Skills. "Litigation" is a generic and vague Skill, while "appellate advocacy" may be more helpful to someone wondering what it is that they might want to hire you for. Completing this section is an opportunity to highlight specific Skills that potential clients (or potential employers) might be seeking. For example, if you teach continuing legal education programs or do other public speaking, add speaking Skills to help those looking for potential speakers find you. Think of Skills as a place to highlight your best strengths and have others vote in agreement that they are, indeed, your best strengths, by endorsing you for those Skills.

LinkedIn allows you to "feature" up to three Skills on your Profile. The "featured" skills are the only ones that can be seen when scrolling through your LinkedIn Profile without clicking on "Show more." You can choose the three Skills to feature, or LinkedIn will choose the three Skills with the highest number of endorsements by default. You can change the featured Skills and reorder all of the Skills on your profile by clicking on the edit (pencil) icon in the Skills and Endorsements section of your Profile. Here, you can delete outdated or unwanted Skills, or drag and drop Skills to change the order they are shown on your Profile. You can also change your Endorsement settings by clicking on the "Adjust endorsement settings" button. Don't forget to click the blue Save button to save your changes!

The Endorsement settings are on-off toggle buttons that allow you to choose how endorsements work on your Profile—you can choose to turn them off entirely, turn off the ability for LinkedIn to show endorsement suggestions to your connections, or turn off the setting that shows you suggestions to endorse your connections. We discuss settings in more detail in Chapter 3.

Making Your Profile Complete

As you build your LinkedIn Profile, LinkedIn will keep track of your Profile Strength and give you hints about what you should do to improve it. The Profile Strength Meter will show you how strong your Profile is and provide suggestions. By clicking on the drop-down in the upper right corner of the Profile Strength Meter, you'll see LinkedIn's recommendations for next steps you can take to improve your Profile to make it more visible in search results.

If your Profile has reached the maximum strength ("All Star"), you'll no longer see the Profile Strength Meter, and you will be given the option to share your Profile on Facebook or Twitter, which might help you draw new visitors to your Profile. You will also see the "All-Star" designation on the top right of your Dashboard on your Profile.

Your goal is a Profile that is considered 100 percent complete. To reach 100 percent completeness, your Profile should contain at least:

- ► Your photo
- ► Your industry and location
- ► Your Summary/About Section
- ► Your current position, with a description
- ► Two past positions
- ► Your education
- ► At least 5 skills (keep the ethical issues discussed in Chapter 28 in mind!)
- ► Fifty or more connections

We recommend that you spend some time completing your Profile, but it does not need to be done in one sitting. If you commit to spending only fifteen minutes or so per day completing the basic sections mentioned in this chapter, you will have a completed Profile in a few days without feeling overwhelmed.

Once you have finished your Profile, you can print it or export it as a PDF (*http://help.linkedin.com/app/answers/detail/a_id/4281*). This might be useful to get an up-to-date print resume to someone who needs it quickly.

Even when your Profile shows that LinkedIn considers you an All Star, there are additional steps you can take to make your Profile more robust, more searchable, and more effective for reaching your LinkedIn goals. To learn how to do that, let us move to Chapter 7.

7

GOING FURTHER WITH YOUR PROFILE

N ow that your basic Profile has been completed and you are more familiar with the LinkedIn interface, let's talk about making your Profile really stand out. There are several good reasons to have as complete a Profile as possible on LinkedIn.

LinkedIn as a Marketing Tool

First and foremost, your LinkedIn Profile is a marketing document. It is your online ambassador working for you twenty-four hours a day. If potential clients or referral sources find you on LinkedIn, you want them to have as much information about you at their fingertips as possible, and you want it to present you in the best light possible. The more comprehensive your Profile, the more reasons people have to connect or engage with you.

Improved Search Engine Visibility

Second, a Profile containing details about you and your practice areas will improve your online visibility. When people have been referred to you or already know your name, they are likely to vet you online by conducting a Google search. Your LinkedIn Profile may be the first result they see in a long list of search results.

Even if the individual searching does not already have your name, the more information you have available in your Profile, the better your chances of appearing in the search engines for relevant terms because LinkedIn is so large and so optimized for search. Provide content on your Profile that includes relevant keywords that potential clients and referral sources might use to search for a lawyer or for information in your practice area or area of expertise.

Increased Visibility and Discoverability on LinkedIn

Third, the more complete your Profile, the more likely it is that your Profile will be found by searches *within* LinkedIn. LinkedIn indicates that users with complete Profiles might be up to forty times more likely to receive opportunities through LinkedIn than those with incomplete Profiles. As you will see later in this book, LinkedIn has robust search capabilities, but you cannot be found if your information is not there.

The LinkedIn search algorithm uses your Profile to determine your relevance to others searching on the site for companies, Connections, or individuals with particular skills or experience. Even if you *are* found, it is much more likely that someone will want to connect or engage with you if your Profile is complete. Missing information can be frustrating to other LinkedIn users. Completeness demonstrates that you take care in presenting yourself to others and that you are willing to share useful information.

Reputation Management and Personal Branding

Fourth, a completed Profile helps you manage your reputation online. Whether you work for yourself or are part of a firm, you have a personal brand. Perhaps you do not have your own website or blog or you work for a firm that does not have a satisfactory web presence or content online. You can still build your personal brand through LinkedIn and provide others, including strategic alliances, potential referral sources, and potential employers, with a comprehensive view of your professional skills and capabilities. You cannot always control what others might say about you on the Internet, but you can take control of your message on LinkedIn and provide high-quality content that demonstrates your expertise. Why squander the opportunity? (We talk more about building your personal brand in Chapter 22).

Finding the Right Job

Fifth, if you are a legal professional in search of a job, your LinkedIn Profile may be just as important as—if not more important than—your resume. At a minimum, it is a resume that it is out working for you twenty-four hours a day, available to anyone who might be interested in hiring you. LinkedIn's Resume Builder tool (***http://resume.linkedinlabs.com***) can even help you generate an up-to-date printed résumé from your LinkedIn Profile.

We discuss the use of LinkedIn for job search in more detail in Chapter 23.

Improving Your Profile

To continually improve your Profile over time, click on the dropdown at the top right of the Profile Strength Meter we discussed in the previous chapter. Or click on the blue "Add profile section" button that appears at the bottom of your Introduction Card when you view your Profile and that remains at the top of the page as you scroll down your Profile. On the mobile app, the blue circle with the white plus sign will move with you at the bottom right of your screen as you scroll down your Profile—click that circle to add to or update your Profile.

Adding Profile Sections

There are many different sections you can add to your Profile. We'll discuss the ones we think are most relevant to legal professionals here. Several of those sections appear in the Accomplishments section. These include:

Honors & Awards

This section is where you'll list any honors you've received, including being named a Super Lawyer, being named pro bono attorney of the year, or other professional honors and awards. LinkedIn sorts honors and awards in alphabetical and chronological order. If there is no date, it will display at the bottom of the section.

Publications

Published books and articles, whether in print or online, add to your credibility and help establish your expertise by demonstrating what you know and how you can help others. LinkedIn allows you to list the title, publication, date, a brief description, as well as a link to the content if it is online. These are automatically sorted in reverse chronological order. If there is no date, the publication will automatically appear at the bottom of the list.

Licenses and Certifications

If you're certified in a particular area of the law or specialty, this is an important section to add to your Profile; it will help you to stand out, and in many jurisdictions, having specific certifications entitles you to call yourself an expert or indicate that you specialize in a particular area. Certifications are automatically displayed in chronological order. If there is no date, it will display at the bottom.

Some lawyers may wish to add their bar admissions information to this section of their Profile, as Dennis has done.

Projects

The Projects subsection can be another place for legal professionals to discuss some information that might not naturally fit elsewhere on your Profile. For example, if you worked on a big case (subject to ethics rules), this might be a place to put that information. Allison has her books listed both in Projects and in Publications on her Profile because she has fewer items that fit into the Projects category and wants to highlight the books. Projects are sorted in alphabetical and chronological order. If there is no date, the item will display at the bottom.

Organizations

The Organizations subsection lets you list organizations you belong to or are affiliated with, but not employed by. This is the place you might list things like bar association leadership or committee positions, board memberships and the like. Like other sections under Accomplishments, entries in this section are sorted in chronological order. If there is no date, the item will display at the bottom.

Volunteer Experience

Many lawyers are active in their local community, house of worship, school district or other volunteer or charity organization. Not only can these experiences be another indication of leadership skills, but they can be another potential source of connections. So, if you are a little league coach, volunteer at your local food pantry, or organize a local group collecting clothes for the homeless, include it on your LinkedIn Profile.

Languages, Test Scores, and Courses

As the world becomes increasingly global, the ability to communicate with those who speak other languages will become more and more important. Many clients choose a lawyer specifically because the lawyer can understand them in their native language, without the need for a third party to act as an interpreter. Languages are automatically displayed alphabetically.

Law students or recent graduates might also consider adding the Test Scores and Courses subsections to showcase their interests, experiences and accomplishments in law school.

Organizing or Rearranging Your Profile

Although LinkedIn has removed the ability to rearrange the order the different sections appear on your Profile, you can rearrange items *within* certain sections on your Profile to put the most relevant information in a more prominent position or closer to the top of the section.

You can rearrange the items within these sections on your Profile:

- ► Experience (current positions only)
- ► Education
- ► Volunteer experience
- ► Skills and Endorsements

Adding Multimedia Elements to Your Profile

In addition to text, you can add images, videos, and presentations to your LinkedIn Profile in the About, Experience, and Education sections. This can be done either by uploading the files directly to LinkedIn or by adding a link to those items on a third-party site.

In the Edit Profile screen for any of those three sections, scroll to the end of the section where it says "Media" and then either click to upload the media from your computer or click link to link to the location of that media online.

You can add a title and description to files you have uploaded. Other users can "like" or comment on the work you have uploaded. Adding media to your Profile is a good way to make it stand out from others, but it is also an excellent way to demonstrate the skills, knowledge and experience that you talk about elsewhere in your Profile.

Writing Your Profile to Encourage Connections

When developing your LinkedIn Profile, think about your purpose for joining LinkedIn (what you are hiring LinkedIn to do for you) and who you would like to connect with on the platform. You may have several "target audiences," including referral sources, strategic partners, potential clients, existing clients and colleagues. If you want those people to connect with you, keep them in mind when developing your Profile.

Continuously update your Profile and tweak the language so that it resonates better with your target audience(s). For example, if a lay person reviewed your LinkedIn Profile, would they immediately know what you actually *do* for your clients? Would they be able to recognize who to refer to you or, if they are potential clients themselves, would they be able to identify themselves as people who would definitely need your services just from reading your Profile? Does your Profile discuss the benefits that your clients receive from working with you? Does it demonstrate that you understand your clients and their problems?

Write in the first person, as if you are speaking directly to your audience. This will help build rapport. Encourage people to connect with you by telling them directly in your Profile how you can be of service to them.

Updating and Maintaining Your Profile

Your LinkedIn Profile isn't a "one and done" proposition; it is something that needs to be kept up to date, which means it requires periodic updating and maintenance. We recommend that you revisit your Profile at least every 6 months to ensure that it is accurate and up to date, even if you haven't made any big changes to your career. As your career evolves and you gain more experience, your Profile should evolve with it.

Your Headline, About, and current Position should be regularly updated to reflect what you are doing right now, who you are doing it for, and what current projects you are undertaking. You might find that some links are broken or that you prefer to highlight different information on your Profile, or even that you want to change some of the keywords you use to describe what you do.

Here are some other occasions when your Profile should be updated:

- ► Beginning a job with a new firm or organization
- ► Changing your title or status with your firm or organization (for example, when you make partner)
- ► Adding or eliminating a practice area
- ► Receiving an honor or award
- ► Publishing a new book or article
- ► Acquiring a new skill
- ► Obtaining a new certification
- ► Joining a new organization
- ► Taking on a leadership role (for example, taking on a Chair position on a Bar Association Committee, joining the Board of a charitable organization, etc.)
- ► Speaking at or attending an important event (adding images, video, etc. to your Profile)

When making changes to your Profile, you may want to consider whether you want your LinkedIn Network to receive notification of those changes. It can be uncomfortable to receive "congratulations" messages from colleagues about a "new" position if you are just tweaking your Headline. If you are making a lot of changes to your Profile at once, you may not want to risk your Connections getting multiple messages about your changes.

Often, we recommend that when legal professionals are making a lot of changes to their Profile, or making changes that are not substantive (in other words, changing their Headline without actually changing jobs or getting a new position), that they turn off those notifications in their Settings (you can read more about Settings in Chapter 3). But since notification of substantive changes is a valuable way to stay in touch with your network, stay "top of mind" and keep them up to date about what you are doing and where you are now, you'll want to make sure that you go back and change your settings again when you are finished.

LinkedIn Analytics and Refining Your Strategy

In addition to the hints that LinkedIn provides you to improve your Profile strength, the Dashboard contains other analytics and information that can help you improve your Profile and function as part of the feedback loop we discussed earlier in this book. We also discuss analytics in Chapter 18.

Who's Viewed Your Profile

LinkedIn will not only tell you how many people have viewed your Profile over the past 90 days within the Dashboard, but clicking on this number will take you to another screen containing additional analytics. This is one of the places that having one of the LinkedIn premium accounts can make a difference.

If you have a free account, LinkedIn will provide you with the number of people who have viewed your Profile, as well as an indication of trends over the past week, whether views of your Profile are increasing or decreasing, as well as a chart to visualize this information. With a free account you will also get some limited additional analytics and information about who has viewed your Profile. For example, you might get information that several of your views have come from people who all work for a specific company, in a particular industry, or have a particular title.

By contrast, if you have one of the premium accounts, such as Sales Navigator or Premium Business, you will get more information. For more details on the extra features you get with premium accounts, see Chapter 1.

Keep in mind, however, that you will never get *all* of the information about *everyone* who views your Profile since some of those people may have indicated in their own settings on LinkedIn that they wish to remain anonymous. LinkedIn will not violate this setting, even for paid premium account holders.

Post Views

The Dashboard will also tell you how many people have viewed your posts on LinkedIn. Clicking on this number brings up your post activity page on LinkedIn, listing your posts and showing the engagement received by each post, in likes, comments and shares. We'll talk more about posting and engagement later in the book when we discuss the third building block of LinkedIn, Participation, but for now, let's look at this information from the point of view of improving your Profile.

The amount of engagement your posts receive can give you some insights about how to improve your Profile and what your target audience is interested in, which can help you to update your Profile to include what is most interesting and engaging to your audience.

Search Appearances

Finally, your Dashboard will show you the number of times you have appeared in LinkedIn Search in the past week. Clicking on that number will bring you to another screen which provides insights into who is searching: where they work, what they do, and what keywords they use to search.

Again, this information can be used to improve your Profile. For example, are you appearing in search for people who fit into your target audience? Are the keywords being searched keywords that you want to be known for? Do those keywords accurately describe what you do? Make adjustments accordingly.

Now that you understand why it's so important to have a complete, up-to-date Profile, and you have moved beyond the basic Profile by adding sections, writing with your target audience(s) in mind, and are using the information provided by your Network in the form of engagement with your Profile and your posts, in the next chapter, we'll cover some Profile tips for LinkedIn power users.

8

ADVANCED AND POWER USER TIPS: PROFILE

As we mentioned in the previous two chapters, your LinkedIn Profile, like your career, will grow and change over time. Here are some additional tips to help you take your Profile to the next level.

In addition to your Profile photo, you can add a banner/header photo to your Profile. This is a frequently-missed opportunity to reinforce your brand and to provide a visual representation of your value and what you do. Your image can represent the type of law you practice, and/or it can include your logo and/or other contact information. The photo should be 1584 x 396 pixels, or at least in a 4:1 ratio.

Take a look at the Profiles of some power users to see how they're maximizing their LinkedIn presence. How do their Profiles look different than yours? What elements do they include? How are they engaging visitors?

Add some interest to your Profile. Make your experience come alive. Your Profile should be interesting and entertaining, not read like a flat, boring resume. Inject some personality. Use stories or examples to illustrate what you do for clients or to provide additional insight.

Include keywords. LinkedIn has great SEO "juice" on the regular search engines like Google, but it also has its own powerful built-in search engine, and business owners and other professionals use LinkedIn's search feature to find and connect with professionals they want to do business with. If your Profile doesn't include the keywords they're looking for, you won't get noticed.

Your LinkedIn analytics can help you to refine your keywords. If you look at the analytics for the number of times you appeared in search, you can see the keywords that people were searching for. Are they the keywords you want to be known for? Do they match with the Skills you have listed on your Profile? Does your Profile include who you help and how you help them? If not, make some changes.

Name your target audience in your Profile and speak their language. Don't fill your Profile with acronyms and legalese unless you're sure that your audience understands and appreciates it. Use the language your clients use to describe their legal problems. Don't be a cliché: every business says they are a 'quality' company where 'service is a top priority.' It's a joke in the legal industry that all firms are "full-service" firms practicing in literally every legal practice area that has ever been or will be invented. Instead, demonstrate your message: show, don't tell.

Add relevant, appropriate video, audio, presentations, or other extras to showcase your work and what you do for clients.

Keep your Profile fresh—switch out the media that is displayed. Change or update your About section to add new experiences. Post images on your profile from speaking engagements, networking events, charity and community participation. Update your Skills or move the most relevant Skills to the "Featured" section. Remove outdated information, documents or publications to make way for more recent or more relevant information.

Add your admissions information to your About, Experience or Licenses and Certifications sections of your Profile to make it clear where you practice.

Add a call to action to your About section, and include your contact information to make it easier for visitors to contact you. Not everyone on LinkedIn will know how to get to your contact info in the Introduction Card. The call to action could be a link to your website, an invitation to download a book or checklist, or simply an invitation to contact you for an initial consultation.

To make your Profile stand out and make it easier to read, use bullet points and short, not long paragraphs. Break your About section and Positions into sections.

Compose your entries in a word processing program, then copy and paste into LinkedIn.

Review your Profile on both the desktop and mobile app versions of LinkedIn to see what information appears before the "see more" link. On the mobile app, you will see just how important the Headline and the first 20-25 words of your About section are; they are the only descriptions you see when scrolling through a Profile on the app; everywhere else there is a description requires additional clicks.

Click on "Add Profile Section" periodically to see if LinkedIn has added new sections that might be relevant to you.

9

PROFILE FREQUENTLY ASKED QUESTIONS

How often should I update my Profile?

We recommend that you update your Profile any time you make a significant change in your career, such as a job change, adding a new practice area, or acquiring a new Skill. But you should also update your Profile when you write a new article or create new media that you can add. As a general rule, even if you think nothing new has happened, you should do a thorough review of your Profile at least every 6 months to see if it needs to be updated.

Should I include all of my previous employment on my Profile, even if some of my positions have nothing to do with the law or what I'm doing now?

As always, the answer to this question may differ depending on what you are hiring LinkedIn to do for you and where you are on your career.

Including your entire employment history on your Profile can help you in several different ways. First of all, connecting with previous employers by including them on your Profile can make you more visible to other current and former employees of the same company or organization. In addition, failing to include all of your employment could result in some gaps in your employment history on your Profile, which could be a red flag for some people.

Think about the skills or experiences you gained in a particular position. Even if it doesn't have anything to do with the law or with what you are doing now, those experiences could be potentially valuable to a potential employer, referral source or client. For example, one of the partners in Allison's old firm liked to hire lawyers who had worked in restaurants because he felt that the people skills learned in that industry translated well into the legal field.

Showing all of your employment history gives a good, well-rounded picture of who you are as a human being, not just as a lawyer, and may help establish connections with other LinkedIn users.

What kinds of multi-media elements should I include on my Profile?

LinkedIn provides you with opportunities to demonstrate your skills and your knowledge by allowing multi-media elements in your About, Experience and Education sections. Some examples of multi-media elements that you can highlight include:

- ► A photo of you with your colleagues at a bar association event (although not as your main Profile photo)

- ► A short video giving a tip about why you need a prenuptial agreement

- ► A PDF checklist for new home buyers on what to think about when purchasing their first house

- ► An infographic showing the pros and cons of using a trust in your estate plan
- ► The slides from a recent CLE presentation

Should I include my contact information on my Profile?

This is a matter of personal preference, but in most cases, we recommend that you include contact information on your Profile if you want to get the most out of LinkedIn and give users a way to connect with you outside of the platform. Remember that you can choose in your Settings who can see your email address if you don't to make that information public on LinkedIn. If your purpose is to make connection, build your network, and advance your relationships, providing as many ways to get in touch with you as possible is probably a good strategy.

How do I know what keywords to focus on in my Profile?

Finding the right keywords may involve some trial and error, and the "right" keywords will likely change over time (which is another reason to update your Profile regularly). In general, we recommend that you use keywords or language that your target audience would use to search for someone who does what you do. Don't use legalese or industry acronyms unless it is well-known and regularly used by your target audience. Think about the language that your target audience uses when they talk to you, or how you explain basic concepts in your practice area to potential clients.

What if I don't have a specific target audience in mind?

In most cases, without at least *some* idea who you want to connect with and why, you will have a more difficult time getting results on LinkedIn. Who are your clients? Who generally refers business to you? Who do you want to receive your messages? Who are your services relevant to?

What if I have several different target audiences and/or practice areas? How do I know what to include on my Profile?

It is perfectly acceptable to have more than one audience. You can either choose one to focus on with your LinkedIn Profile or write different items to attract one audience at a time based on their needs, wants or preferences. For example, you might have one paragraph in your About section dedicated to what you do for your clients and another paragraph that discusses how you work with other legal professionals (to key in on referral sources) or describes the topics you speak on (to target organizations seeking speakers). We discuss Company Pages and Showcase pages in Chapter 26. Either of them might be used to present different material to different audiences as well.

Should job seekers include their desired position in their Headline?

If you have a specific kind of job in mind, you can certainly make it clear in your Headline. But be aware that if you are currently employed, your employer or other colleagues may be able to see this information. If you do not want them to know that you are job hunting, you might want to keep that information out of your Headline.

If you don't want your employer to know you're jobhunting, you can still use LinkedIn's job search and apply for jobs listed on LinkedIn, and you can make sure that your Professional Headline and your summary reflect the knowledge, skills and experience that would be attractive to a new potential employer or for the new position that you are seeking. The premium account for job hunters provides some helpful protection to keep your current employer from finding that you are looking for a new job.

What you include in your Headline depends upon what you're looking for, what you think your audience will respond to, and how much attention you want to call to it. If you want to let as many people as possible know that you're seeking a specific kind of position, putting it right up front in your Headline is likely to attract attention. Because networking is so important in finding new jobs, more and more people are announcing that they are looking for something new and asking their Connections for help, with good results.

For example, your Headline might read, "Recent New York Law Grad Seeking Associate Position in Commercial Real Estate."

PART III

CONNECTIONS

10

GETTING STARTED WITH CONNECTIONS

The second essential building block of LinkedIn is Connections. If Profiles answer the "Who are you?" question, Connections answer the "Who do you know?" question. By building a solid LinkedIn network with good Connections, you will create a foundation that will help you get the most value out of the site. LinkedIn offers some great Connection tools to map out and populate your network.

After Microsoft bought LinkedIn in 2016, we (and many others) expected to see a much tighter integration between Outlook contacts and LinkedIn. We still expect that to happen, but the timeframe is uncertain. You can definitely see an emphasis on importing all of your contacts, no matter where you keep them, and new tools to centralize the management of all of your contacts in LinkedIn. LinkedIn has also added some contact management or "customer relationship management" features that users had been asking for over the years, although many of these features are available only with one of LinkedIn's paid subscriptions. Watch for developments in these areas.

Connecting Principles

The easiest way to understand LinkedIn's approach to Connections is to think in terms of "six degrees of separation." The idea, often jokingly associated with the actor Kevin Bacon, who has appeared in many movies, is that if we map our contacts to our contacts' contacts, to our contacts' contacts' contacts, and so on, we will be able to get from any person on the planet to any other person on the planet within six steps. LinkedIn adopts this notion of degrees of separation and will map the steps of relationship from you to anyone else. You will see the degree of separation next to the name of people you encounter on LinkedIn (1st, 2nd, etc.)

Someone directly connected to you is a first-degree Connection. For example, Allison and Dennis are connected on LinkedIn, so we are first degree connections. Someone connected to your first-degree Connection (but not directly to you) is a second-degree Connection. So, if Dennis is connected to you on LinkedIn, but you are not connected to Allison, you and Allison would be second-degree connections—you each have Dennis as a common connection. You will also find third-degree Connections (someone connected to a second-degree Connection of yours). To follow our example, since you and Allison are second-degree connections, someone connected to Allison, but not connected to you or Dennis would be a third-degree connection. Anything beyond a third-degree connection on LinkedIn is designated as "3+".

In the LinkedIn world, you are able to do more with a first-degree Connection than with a second- or third-degree Connection, just as in the real world. For example, only first-degree Connections can endorse you for a Skill on LinkedIn.

For the most part, LinkedIn also uses a "symmetrical" approach to social networking. Social media tools like Twitter (where you "follow" people) an "asymmetrical" approach. In other words, I can follow you even if you do not follow me back. In LinkedIn, the approach is two-way or symmetrical. I can add you as a Connection of mine only if you affirmatively accept my invitation to become a Connection, and vice versa. The result is that there is a confirmed and mutually agreed upon relationship between LinkedIn Connections. We will discuss later the notion of "following," which, if the person you are following permits, will let you see his or her activity, but does not give you the benefits and privileges of a Connection.

Before jumping in to add Connections, you should decide on a strategy or guiding philosophy about how you want to grow your network (quality vs. quantity, local vs. national, real world vs. Internet, internal vs. external, etc.). Checking the number of contacts you have in Outlook or in another address book will be a good place to start in terms of thinking about the approach you want to take on LinkedIn. There is no one-size-fits-all approach on how you should handle connections. In fact, Dennis and Allison use quite different approaches. Your philosophy on adding connections may also change from time to time, especially if you are looking for a new job, starting a new practice area, or changing geographies.

Getting Off to a Running Start

LinkedIn now has great tools for adding Connections. If your experience with LinkedIn dates back several years, you will be pleasantly surprised at how much easier it has become to add people. In the early days, adding Connections often involved several e-mails where you needed to explain to invitees what LinkedIn was and then wait for them to set up their own accounts. Put those bad memories out of your mind.

In this chapter, we will show you two standard ways to add contacts to your LinkedIn network. Use both of these regularly (not just once), based on what seems to work best for you. Many legal professionals begin with LinkedIn but never add more than a handful of Connections. If you fall into that category or are new to LinkedIn, these tips will help you get off to a running start. Even if you already have a substantial list of Connections, we recommend that you supplement your list with these two techniques.

In the current version of LinkedIn, most of the work that you will do with connections will become available by clicking on the My Network tab on the top navigation bar, or clicking on the Network icon (it looks like people) at the bottom of the screen on the mobile app. Remember that LinkedIn constantly changes specific elements of its interface to improve its user experience, so specific details might have changed from what you read here, but you should be able to see how to do these things relatively easily if LinkedIn has made changes.

Mining Your Contacts—The Automated Approach

Importing existing contacts is a great way to get started with Connections. LinkedIn makes it very easy to coordinate your Connections with your current contacts in Outlook, other contact programs, or other webmail accounts. By populating your Connections from the start with a good number of contacts from your current address book, you can quickly see how LinkedIn works and might benefit you.

LinkedIn allows you to pull in your connections from Outlook and a number of other web services (Gmail, Yahoo, etc.). Simply navigate the instructions and LinkedIn will import those connections for you. You can either do this by entering your account information, with password, or manually importing your Outlook connections. LinkedIn will walk you through the process.

Note that LinkedIn has realized that most people are sensitive about uploading their contacts to LinkedIn and what LinkedIn might be able to do with them. LinkedIn states that its use is quite limited and tries to reassure you.

Once you import your contacts, you will see a page currently titled "Connect with people you know on LinkedIn." It will be a list of the people in your contacts who are on LinkedIn, but who are not first-degree connections.

Each imported contact will have a check box by his or her name. To invite someone you have imported to be your first-degree Connection, simply check the box by the person's name. We strongly recommend that you uncheck "select all" at the top left and go through the imported list to individually check names.

After you have selected your invitees, click on the link to send the invitations, and wait to receive notifications from the people who accept. This method is a powerful and fast way to add a lot of people you already know as Connections or to conveniently update your current list. (If you forgot to uncheck "select all" and have accidentally sent invitations to your entire address book, don't panic! We show you how to withdraw those invitations in Chapter 17)

One drawback of using this bulk approach is that you cannot use personalized invitations to your contacts. Personalized invitations have long been the preferred approach, so this might be an issue. Your best contacts might not appreciate a generic approach, and other contacts might not remember who you are.

These reasons are also why we do not recommend leaving all the boxes checked when you import your contacts or sending invitations to everyone you have imported, which LinkedIn makes far too easy to do. On the other hand, use of LinkedIn is so prevalent today that it might not bother anyone to receive the default LinkedIn invitation. However, you will miss the opportunity to make a warm and personalized invitation. You will need to make the judgment call.

Personalized Invitations

As we said above, in most situations, we recommend personalizing your invitations to connect on LinkedIn rather than using the default LinkedIn invitation wording. Some people can get a little touchy about getting the default invitation from someone they know. They might also be reluctant to connect with you if they don't know who you are or why you want to connect. There are some indications that these attitudes are relaxing, but if your main goal is to establish meaningful connections that could lead to other opportunities—in other words, to establish relationships—sending a personalized invitation is preferred.

A word of warning: in the LinkedIn mobile app, it is still too easy to send a non-personalized invitation before you realize that you have done so. As we said elsewhere, that might be because of the belief that you will be using the mobile app to connect with someone you are standing beside. In today's era of using mobile apps for everything, that assumption might no longer be a good one.

A personalized invitation is preferred especially if you have already established some connection with the individual you are inviting to connect with you on LinkedIn—for example, if you've already met in person, if you have something in common, such as belonging to the same groups, having a mutual connection, and the like. A personalized invitation is a great way to remind the person who you are, how you know them, or to say thank you, all of which make it easy for the invitee to accept your invitation. After all, if you're sending an invitation to Connect, your goal, regardless of the reason you want to connect with this person, is for them to accept your invitation, whether you know them already or not. Why not make it easy for them by reminding them how you know them or why it would be beneficial for them to connect with you?

To send a personalized invitation go to that person's Profile and click the blue Connect button. You will be asked if you want to add a note or send the invitation without a note. Choose the adding a note option and you get a maximum of 300 characters to create your personalized invitation. If you've done a search on the person's name and they've come up in the search results, you can click Connect next to their information right in the search results to create your personalized invitation.

Personalizing your invitations doesn't need to be time consuming or complicated, and the extra effort goes a long way in establishing or strengthening relationships and demonstrates that you are someone worth connecting with. Saying something as simple as "It was great to meet you at the breast cancer fundraiser last night" will help people remember you and make them more likely to add you as a Connection and even reply personally to you, moving the relationship forward.

The option to personalize invitations to connect is available in the LinkedIn mobile app, but, as we mentioned, it is far too easy to send an invitation without a personalized invitation. If you touch the blue "Connect" button, the invitation is immediately sent. You need to tap the "More" button and then use the "Personalize invite" option.

Keep in mind that if you use the People You May Know feature we will talk about in the next chapter to locate potential connections, the option to personalize your invitation is not available on the mobile app. Clicking on the Connect button it will send out the default invitation. You can still use the tool to identify potential connections and then hover over the person you want to connect with and click on View Profile to navigate to their Profile, and then click Connect from there to personalize your invitation as outlined above.

You should already be getting the idea that there is no excuse for having only a tiny number of Connections on LinkedIn. These two basic techniques will give you a great start. In the next chapter, we show you more powerful tools to build your network.

11

MAKING EVEN MORE CONNECTIONS

I n Chapter 10, we showed you the two most basic ways to build your network of Connections: uploading existing contacts and sending personalized invitations from someone's Profile. While you can go a long way using just those two techniques, you will be using only a tiny fraction of the potential power of the LinkedIn connecting tools.

In this chapter, we discuss some of the connecting tools and techniques that we like best. We also highlight the importance of treating the development of your Connections list as an evolving process that you should pay attention to on a regular basis. As your list of Connections grows, you will notice the variety of powerful ways that LinkedIn gives you to filter, sort, and add to it and become more valuable as your connections grow. These tools can be quite useful and will encourage you to add more Connections.

Here are five essential methods for adding more high-quality Connections. These techniques leverage the power of LinkedIn second-degree Connections. In simplest terms, you will be trying to convert second-degree connections into first-degree connections. We will give even more power techniques in Chapter 13.

Groups

We recommend joining Groups as an effective way to network through LinkedIn. Joining LinkedIn Groups similar to the groups and organizations you belong to in real life or that are organized around your interests or your clients' interests is a good way to start. Or you can look at the Groups some of your best connections belong to; if your ideal client belongs to a particular Group, perhaps other potential clients belong as well. (We'll talk more about Groups in Chapter 15).

LinkedIn Groups can be a good source of Connections, particularly as you learn more about people and engage with them in discussions through the Group. Once you belong to a Group, you exponentially expand your ability to connect with others. LinkedIn lets you to send free messages to those who are in your Groups even if you are not a first-degree connection, without using up your InMail credits. (See the Participation section of this book for more information on sending messages through LinkedIn.)

To send invitations to Group members, navigate to the Group, find the person you want to connect with and hover over their name. Click the envelope icon that appears to send a message to them. While this won't generate an invitation to connect, it will start the conversation, and you can choose to send an invitation later. Or perhaps that person will invite you to connect once they receive your message.

Alternatively, you can click on the person's name from the Group list, which will bring you to their Profile. Then click the Connect button to send an invitation. If you share a Group with a potential connection, you have a somewhat expanded ability to invite them to connect—in general, LinkedIn will always permit you to send an invitation to a second level connection, but may not always allow you to invite a third level connection. However, if you and a third level connection are both members of the same Group, LinkedIn will usually allow you to invite them to connect without asking you for any additional information.

Alumni

For many people, the most productive form of affiliation connections are alumni relationships, especially if you went to a small college or a university with a strong alumni network (e.g., Notre Dame). This is true even if you did not know fellow alumni personally or did not graduate in the same class. Think for a moment about how likely you are to help out someone who went to the same college as you did. Our guess is that if you get a LinkedIn invitation from someone who is a fellow alumna/alumnus of your school, your instinct will be to accept that invitation.

LinkedIn has long recognized what a rich source of quality connections school affiliations are and has made it very easy to find and reach out to those people. Simply go to the My Network tab on the navigation bar and click it.

You will see a whole dashboard with information about your Connections and network. This dashboard has been changing recently, so keep an eye on it for further developments. On this page you will see a section called "`School alumni you may know" and names and photos of alumni LinkedIn suggests as possible Connections. There is also a link called "See all." Click on that and you will see all the suggestions and you can simply click on the Connect button to add the ones that make sense for you.

Go to the search box and enter the name of your school. Click on the name of the school you want in the search results. You will be taken to a page for the school. One of the choices (currently in the left column menu) is "Alumni." Click on that button and many alumni connection options will appear.

You can search alumni by location, title or company. You can specify a year or range of years of attendance and apply filters such as the years they attended, what they do for a living, where they work, and more.

The way these features work is self-explanatory, but we want to highlight a few great features. First, you can search for people who graduated in the same year you did. You can also search for people in a range of years. This is convenient way to find people who were at school in the years you were there, but not in the same class. The year range feature can be helpful if you are looking to reach out to a targeted area of alumni, such as those who graduated in the last five years or alumni at retirement age or older. It's also easy to shift from school to school. You can even get some demographic information. Try to resist the urge to check up on old boyfriends, girlfriends or archrivals and focus on your purpose and strategy.

Once you find people to connect to, you can go to their Profiles and invite them to connect. A simple personal invitation will be highly effective here.

Former Work Colleagues

Another rich source of professional contacts that you might have lost touch with are your former work colleagues. Again, LinkedIn makes it easy to connect with these people. Simply go to the My Network tab on the navigation bar and click it.

On this page you will see a section called "People you may have worked with" and photos of people LinkedIn suggests as possible Connections. There is also a link called "See all." Click on that and you will see all the suggestions and you can simply click on the Connect button to add the ones that make sense for you.

For more suggestions, similar to the way you searched for alumni, go to the search box and enter the name of the firm, company or organization where you previously worked. Click on the name of the company you want in the search results. You will be taken to a page for the firm or company, and you can click on the link to see all employees. For companies, you are limited to current employees, making it less useful than the alumni options, but it can still be a good resource.

Once you find people to connect to, you can go to their Profiles and invite them to connect. A simple personal invitation will be highly effective here.

Advanced Search Emphasizing Second Degree Connections

We will discuss LinkedIn's impressive set of advanced search features or "filters" in detail in the next chapter. You can generate very granular search results by checking boxes and typing search terms. If you are targeting certain types of connections, for example, at a company or in a certain city or country, these features can be very valuable. Here, we want to emphasize the simple action of focusing your search results on second-degree Connections.

As an example, you might do a search on your city or a company. When the results appear, you will see a number of filtering options across the top of the page. One is "Connections." Drop down the menu and check the box for second-degree connections. You now have a great list to look through for potential new Connections.

People You May Know

Since its beginnings, LinkedIn has been analyzing connections between people. One of the ways LinkedIn has put what it has learned to use is the "People You May Know" or "More suggestions for you" feature, available under the My Network tab. The idea with this technique is to use and leverage what LinkedIn has learned over the years about networks and Connections.

You can use this feature as a way to find and add Connections. You simply look through the suggestions. LinkedIn shows the numbered of Connections you share. You can simply send an invitation to the ones that interest you or meet your criteria. Remember your strategic plan.

We've been experimenting with this feature in ways that have challenged some of our most fundamental assumptions about LinkedIn—namely that personalized invitations are always best and that it makes the most sense to connect with people you actually know. As a result, we want to suggest that a well-thought-out approach to using People You May Know might be a great way to add large numbers of connections in a strategic (or tactical) way.

Here's the experiment. Again, it's based on the assumption that LinkedIn's network analytics know more than we do.

At any given time, People You May Know will give you hundreds of suggestions. For the most part, those suggestions stay fairly static during the day, but there appears to be a big daily refresh at the end of each day. The experiment requires using People You May Know aggressively on a regular basis, even daily, for a while. This consistent effort will help you see patterns and explore potential directions you can go.

You then decide on a few criteria and filters for making your decision to try connecting to people, based on your purpose. You might focus on geography, job title, employer, et al. Or you might make actually knowing or having met a person a requirement for inviting them to connect. Another criteria might be whether someone has a photo or not. We also recommend using the number of shared connections as a filter.

In addition to a number of purpose-related criteria, Dennis experimented with requiring a minimum of ten shared connections before sending an invitation because he thought he would be likely to accept an invitation from someone with overlapping interests if there were at least ten shared connections. In the experiment, he used the default, non-personalized message for the invitations.

We were very surprised by the results. The biggest surprise was how positive the results were. The acceptance rate was very high. There was a good response from people who followed-up with a personal reply. As Dennis's People You May Know page updated each day, the suggestions improved, and patterns started to reveal themselves. It also became apparent how to build out connections into areas of interest, companies or geographies.

Other unexpected benefits included seeing who in Dennis' own network were often shared connections with many people, Groups that people commonly shared, job titles used for certain jobs, and much more. Perhaps the best learning was how important the short description in your Profile really is. You can see many benefits for a job search, but, keeping your purpose in mind, you may see benefits in other areas as well.

Note that People You May Know can be used in two ways. The first is the focused and personal approach where you find someone, go to their Profile and connect with a personalized invitation. This will be a slow process, especially if you want to add a lot of connections in a short period of time.

You can also scroll through the suggestions on a regular basis and connect with people who interest you. This approach shows the potential of helping you add a good number of quality contacts in a short time. However, we definitely recommend this as an experimental approach and one which you are willing to adapt and make changes to.

A fascinating aspect of this approach is how you grow to trust LinkedIn's analytics and trust the results without trying to understand what you, as a human might think the pattern should be. A second aspect is the potential value of "weak links." Using People You May Know to connect with people that you, well, *don't* know, will certainly result in a weak link rather than a strong link. People who look at networks have stressed the value of weak links. In this case, the weakness of the link might work well as a warm introduction ("We're already connected on LinkedIn") and present the possibility of being granted a small favor. Remember how you tend to help a fellow alum even though you do not know them at all.

Please note that your mileage may vary. Dennis has been on LinkedIn for many years and has a fairly large number of good connections. This starting point might have allowed LinkedIn's algorithms to give better People You May Know results. In addition, his number of connections made it likely to see a significant number of shared connections. If you try this approach, you will definitely need to treat it as a science experiment. Remember that there can be downsides to connecting with people you don't know on LinkedIn. For example, becoming a first-degree connection with someone opens the door to allow them to more easily message you or to endorse your skills even though they don't know what you do.

Connecting Is an Ongoing Process

You can see that LinkedIn offers easy-to-use, powerful tools to get your network off to a fast start and include people who really should be added. However, do not stop after the initial use of these tools. You will continue to meet people. People will want to connect with you. Your networks, both online and in the real world, will continue to grow and evolve. We recommend that you set aside a little time throughout the year to use some of these methods to update your LinkedIn network and make it even more valuable.

Our advice is to start building your network with people you know reasonably well and to whom you want to be connected and learn to work on LinkedIn with those Connections. Then gradually grow your Connections in an organic way, much as you do in the real world. Users' approaches and the number of Connections in their networks will vary. For example, Dennis has a large number of Connections, but that does not mean that his number is a good number for you. Many of his Connections come from his writing and speaking audiences, and, most important, he has been on LinkedIn for more than ten years, slowly adding Connections by using the techniques we have discussed.

12

USING LINKEDIN SEARCH TOOLS

O nce you have uploaded your contacts and have begun sending (and accepting) invitations to connect on LinkedIn, it is time to begin using LinkedIn as a tool to build your practice and broaden your network. Aside from job hunting, professionals use LinkedIn mostly for keeping in touch, industry networking, and promoting their businesses and their expertise. As a result, the site contains a potential gold mine of information about your Connections and possible contacts. Use LinkedIn's robust search engine to find future Connections or to identify potential clients, referral sources, and industry contacts.

Searching by Name

The easiest way to begin looking for people is searching by name. Type the name into the quick search box in the top center of the top navigation bar on every page. As you type, LinkedIn will begin giving you "suggestions" that will appear under the quick search box. If you see the person you are searching for in the suggestions, click directly on that person's name when it appears. These suggestions might or might not be all that useful, but they can often be a good first step.

If you do not use the suggestions LinkedIn provides in the drop-down box, continue typing and then press the Enter key (or click on the magnifying glass to the right of the quick search box).

To begin building your network on a manual basis, search for anyone—friends, colleagues and former colleagues, classmates, neighbors, supervisors, sports teammates, church congregation, and so forth.

Using Other Search Filters

As you may have guessed, you can also use the drop-down menu on the quick search box to search Companies, Groups, Messages, Updates, or Jobs. If you do not have a specific name, you can search by keyword, school, or other terms using this search box as well.

The search tools work much as you would expect. You might, however, be surprised how powerful and effective they are.

You can easily see which of your Connections (first or second degree) have a particular Skill or keyword in their Profiles, which Groups discuss the items you are interested in learning about, and which Companies match keyword terms. Click on any of these categories for more information.

This technique might help you find experts or other specialists, such as forensic evaluation specialists or accident reconstructionists, or to find referral sources, such as accountants or legal professionals in other practice areas.

By contrast, clicking directly on a Company (rather than an individual) in the search suggestion list will bring you to the Company's LinkedIn Home page which includes a brief company description, any Connections you have with that company, and a link to the full list of the company's employees.

Taking Advantage of the Power of LinkedIn Search

LinkedIn is filled with high-level business professionals who use it specifically for business networking. Some of these people you might know or might have had contact with but lost touch. Others might be people you want to know or who could be key to bringing in a new account; in the past, you had no way "in." LinkedIn can help you find your way in.

Advanced Search Techniques

Any time you see the ability to filter results using your own defined parameters, you are using LinkedIn's advanced search features. In the 2017 timeframe, LinkedIn moved away from a separate "advanced search" tool that took you to a search dashboard to an integration of the advanced search features into the normal search function. Longtime LinkedIn users often think that "Advanced Search" has disappeared. It hasn't; it's just been integrated into the normal search experience.

When you click in the search box, a menu drops down and lets you choose, if you want, filters for people, jobs, or content. The drop-down menu also shows your most recent searches.

When you do a search from the main search box, LinkedIn will make suggestions about who or what you are looking for as you type. If you see what you want, you can click on the person or item in the drop-down menu without needing to complete the whole name or search term. LinkedIn often will give you options in that drop-down menu to filter by people, companies, or groups, as appropriate. That's a simple implementation of an integrated advanced search functionality.

Let's try it now with the name of a former firm or employer. Type the name into the search box and click enter to see the search results.

Once you visit the page for your search results, you will see that there are many advanced search tools and filters integrated into buttons at the top of the search results page.

When you perform a search this way, LinkedIn will default to showing your People results first. But if you would like to change the focus of your search you can do so by clicking on the dropdown next to People, where you will find options to search All, Jobs, Content, Companies, Schools, or Groups.

You will also see a variety of People filters across the top. Those filter options will change if you move to one of the other scope options (e.g., Companies). The "Connections" button allows you to filter by first-, second-, or third-degree Connections. You can also filter by locations or current companies. To the right on the options is a link for "See all filters." Click on that and you will find an extensive, powerful, and easy-to-use set of advanced search filters all available in one place. You will also see a subtle reminder that you can get even more advanced search features, such as years of experience and company size in the Career and Sales Navigator premium accounts.

You can also get to the advanced search filters before typing in your search terms by clicking on the magnifying glass in the main search box.

Want to learn more? The ever-helpful LinkedIn Help pages have a good set of resources—***https://www.linkedin.com/help/linkedin/answer/302.***

Saving Searches

If you perform the same searches over and over, you can save your search by clicking on the "Create search alert" link at the top of the right column on your search results page. This will help you when you want to update your searches or search for new contacts within the same target market or a regular basis. You can save up to three searches per week with the free version of LinkedIn and have LinkedIn automatically run the search and e-mail you new results. LinkedIn limits the number of saved searches on the free version and seems to be in the process of eliminating that feature from the free version. If you want to save more than three searches, you must upgrade to one of LinkedIn's premium accounts.

Search is an excellent tool to help you find and add Connections. It is also a powerful tool for competitive intelligence about what your competitors and competitors' clients are doing and a great tool to use in the hiring, job search, and sales prospecting process. It's so easy to use and so integrated into the LinkedIn experience that it can be easy to overlook. Keep LinkedIn search at the top of your LinkedIn toolbox.

13

ADVANCED AND POWER USER
TIPS: CONNECTIONS

The other techniques in the section of the book will help you add and manage Connections to build and grow your network. In fact, if you use only those techniques you will be able to take long strides toward your goals. However, in this chapter, we discuss some tools and tips to go even farther down that road.

People Also Viewed

If you go to someone's Profile page, you will notice on the right on the web interface or at the bottom on the mobile app, a list of ten names under the heading "People also viewed." This feature can give you some insight into the person's network and who people look at when searching for that person. However, it's also another place to look for second-degree Connections that can be turned into first-degree Connections. In simplest terms, your friend's Connections will probably more willing to accept your invitation if they know you have the same trusted friend in common.

Converting Your Business Cards

If you have a stack of business cards, go through them and send those people LinkedIn invitations. You know that you already met them in person and exchanged business cards. Now you can change those real-world connections into LinkedIn Connections.

Accepting Invitations

Do not forget this obvious way to build your Connections. You undoubtedly received e-mails with LinkedIn invitations before you became a LinkedIn user and after you set up your account. As you continue to use LinkedIn, you will get invitations to connect to others on a fairly regular basis. You can receive those invitations in your LinkedIn inbox, through an e-mail notification, or both. Accepting some of those pending invitations is another easy way to add Connections. After all, the person already indicated that they want to connect with you.

When you get an invitation, even from someone you know well, do not simply click on the Accept link in the e-mail. Instead, go to the inviter's Profile page and confirm who the person is, see what he or she is doing, and view in particular the shared Connections you have. You can learn some valuable information about relationships within your network. If you are not sure who someone is, seeing shared Connections can help you determine whether to accept an invitation. You might also use the contact information on the inviter's Profile to send an e-mail asking how you know each other and why you might want to connect.

If you know the person or want to engage in a conversation, we recommend answering the invitation with an e-mail or LinkedIn message thanking the person for the invitation, talking about how you might help them, suggesting a follow up call, or even adding some personal comments if you already know them well. If you do not know the person and do not want to connect, click the Ignore button or just do nothing. Regular LinkedIn users are very tolerant of time delays. If you are reluctant to accept an invitation because you think you've waited too long and the person might be upset with your delay, don't worry about it. If the person didn't want to keep the invitation open, they would have withdrawn it.

We also recommend sending the message after you have accepted the invitation (rather than before) because you can message a first-degree connection. If you have only the free account, you can only use LinkedIn's InMail service to send a limited number of messages (three, as of the publication of this book), so you either have to be connected to send a message or upgrade to a premium account.

Finally, remember that you have the option to "follow" someone rather than add them as a Connection. In some cases, you might want to learn more about people and see what they post on LinkedIn before you decide to add them as an actual Connection. You might later go back to the people you are following and "level up" by accepting their original invitation or inviting them to be a Connection.

Find Nearby

In the mobile app is a feature called "Find Nearby" that lets you see people who also have the feature enabled and who are in Bluetooth range. You need to affirmatively opt-in to use this feature and also turn on Bluetooth sharing. When Find Nearby is turned on, other members can discover you, even when you aren't using the LinkedIn mobile app. To prevent other members from discovering you, switch the Find Nearby feature off. If you are at a conference or meeting where people are willing to try the feature, you can ask everyone with the app to turn it on. Everyone will see who else on LinkedIn with feature turned on is present. It then is a simple matter of clicking on people and immediately connecting with them.

Cultivating Connections

While we focus primarily on adding Connections, it's worth noting that you can remove Connections, block people, withdraw invitations, ignore invitations, and otherwise manage invitations and Connections. (We'll talk more about this in the section on Participation, in Chapter 17) Remember that you should feel no obligation to accept all the invitations you receive. Some people "cull" Connections from time to time by removing people they don't know any more or no longer want to be associated with. It's an option. However, remember that people you've known or associated with in the past might one day, out of the blue, send you work, let you know about a job, invite you to speak, or do other beneficial things. And vice versa.

Simply Viewing Profiles

LinkedIn users with premium accounts can see who has viewed their Profiles. Those with free accounts can see a small number of Profile viewers. This is something worth remembering. Some users will look at who has viewed their Profile and send invitations to those people who look interesting to them. It's a subtle approach, but you can view a Profile (e.g., a hiring partner) and see if that person sends you an invitation to connect. You can do the same thing by monitoring who has viewed your own Profile and sending invitations to interesting viewers.

Inviting Invitations

In addition to sending invitations, you can foster invitations to connect in several different ways. Encouraging people to visit your Profile might generate additional invitations. We always suggest that attendees of our seminars and webinars to send us invitations to connect (ideally, with a personalized message telling us how much they loved our presentation). LinkedIn makes it easy to create a "badge" with a link that you can use on your blog, website, or elsewhere. You can add the URL for your LinkedIn Profile on your resume, business card, or stationery. As we mentioned, LinkedIn also lets you create a scannable QR code that you can use on your business card or else so people can go right to your Profile.

Go Premium . . . At Least for a Little While

Don't forget that premium account options have additional features that can help you find and add Connections. You can take advantage of a free 30-day trial and, if you purchase a premium account, you can turn it off at any time. Depending on your goals and strategy, employing a Premium account such as Sale Navigator can be a big help.

Twitter Followers

If you use Twitter, a great technique is to see who follows you on Twitter and, if it makes sense, send them LinkedIn invitations. It's a signal that you acknowledge and respect their follow and want to take your online relationship up a notch by becoming connected on LinkedIn.

Comments and Likes

When you create a Post on LinkedIn (discussed in the Participation section of this book), people can "like" or otherwise react to your post, or they can comment on it. You can see you has liked, commented on or shared your Post. Looking through the second-degree Connections who have liked or comment on your Post can suggest people to add as Connections. If you send the invitation quickly, they are highly likely to accept your invitation.

Conference Speakers and Authors

We are only half joking when we tell people that if they send a personal invitation saying that they like our books, articles, or presentations, we will almost certainly accept their invitations. People love hearing positive feedback. If you sincerely like a presentation or article, let the speaker or author know and ask them to connect. This approach can be a good way to up the level of your Connections and open new doors by being connected to thought leaders.

If you are speaking at a conference, you might also consider inviting other speakers to connect in advance of the conference. This will make it easier to talk with them in person at the event.

It is surprising to us how often speakers do not have LinkedIn Profiles (or other social media accounts) or have a very small number of Connections. A major purpose of speaking and writing is to engage with your audience. Not being present in an up-to-date way on LinkedIn creates a poor impression and sends a negative message about your willingness to interact with your audience.

We are always finding new ways to use LinkedIn to identify potential Connections. Be creative.

14

FREQUENTLY ASKED QUESTIONS: CONNECTIONS

Should I be more concerned about quantity or quality?

Focus on your own strategy and job to be done. Don't compare yourself to others. Your decision about this approach is uniquely personal and is based on your LinkedIn goals and your individual approach. For example, some LinkedIn users want to create as broad a network as possible; in that case, they would focus more on quantity, and will send and accept more invitations. Others want their LinkedIn Network to provide value not just to themselves, but to others in their Network as well. Users with this approach might send and accept fewer invitations, preferring to have more information about each of their Connections, or to know their Connections personally. That said, if you have a very small number of Connections, some people will interpret that as an indication that you don't use LinkedIn. Something to consider.

Many people have told me that I need to have at least 500 Connections. I don't even know 500 people. Is 500 Connections really the minimum?

The number 500 has become the rule of thumb advice many people give about LinkedIn. It's not magic, but often people see 500+

as an indicator or signal that you are an active user of LinkedIn. It's definitely something to consider and we lean toward reaching that number, if it fits your strategy. Using the techniques in this Section make it highly probably that you will get to the 500 number. You know more people than you think well enough to be connected on LinkedIn, which is different than the number of best friends, trusted advisors, and mentors you know, regardless of what side of the quality vs. quantity debate you fall on.

What is Dunbar's number and how does it factor in to how many LinkedIn Connections I have?

In the 1990s, British anthropologist Robin Dunbar proposed a much-debated theory about the limit of people any can maintain stable social relationships with. A stable relationship means one in which you know the other people and how they relate to each other. Commonly, the number used is 150, but sometimes it is given as a range of 100—250. Dunbar's number often comes up in the discussion of social networking. Does that limit also apply in social networks like LinkedIn?

We like to think in terms of "strong" connections and "weak" connections. Dunbar's number makes sense for "strong" connections. Yet, much of business and daily activity happens in the world of "weak" connections—referrals, occasional interactions, group affiliations, and the like. We think that LinkedIn excels in mapping and activating your weak connections. Dunbar's number is one factor you might consider in developing your LinkedIn strategy. Typically, the more you are convinced about Dunbar's number, the more you move to a quality of Connections approach. The more you are interested in leveraging weak connection, the more you will tend toward a quantity of Connections approach.

Should I only connect with other legal professionals? Should I connect with any other legal professionals?

We often hear both of these questions. Our usual answer is to look at what you do in the real world for guidance. Look to your strategy. We do not advocate putting arbitrary limits on who you might or might not connect with. LinkedIn is an extension of real-life networking, so you should be connecting with people from all kinds of industries and professions on LinkedIn, just as you would in real life. Those connections can be potential clients or referral sources. Many of them may be lawyers, who could also be referral sources, whether they are lawyers who practice in different areas of the law or in different jurisdictions, but we would recommend that you expand your network beyond just legal professionals to make a richer network.

Should I connect with people in my firm, company, or organization?

This question is a tricky one. Largely, it will depend on the culture of your organization. Some organizations expect people to connect. The complication, of course, is that if you are looking for a job, it can become apparent to your connections based on your LinkedIn activity. On the other hand, connection to colleagues can be useful when you leave an organization because they will already be on your list of Connections. We suspect that answering this question and coming up with an approach will prove to be one of your more difficult strategic decisions.

Should I connect with my competitors?

We often get asked whether legal professionals should connect with others in the same practice area and jurisdiction because they are afraid that their competition will see what they are doing and copy them. It's easy to forget that many referrals happen because a "competitor" has a conflict and can't do the work for a client. If you do not connect to the "competitor," you will probably lose out on that opportunity. In addition, copying on LinkedIn won't necessarily be effective, particularly if you have your own strategy which is tailored not only to what you do, but to your specific target audience and based on your specific strengths, weaknesses and experience. If someone wants to go to the trouble of finding out what you're doing and copying it, they can probably do it without actually connecting with you on LinkedIn and as easily as checking your website or Googling you. Finally, we often think people are paying more attention to us than they really are, so it's probably not worth over-thinking this issue.

I remember that LinkedIn originally was known as a tool for introducing two people you knew to each other. I'm not sure how to do that anymore. What's the best technique for introducing to people thorough LinkedIn?

The "Share Profile" feature is perfect for this. Go to the Profile of one of the people you want to introduce. If they are a first-degree Connection, you'll see a button labeled "Message" and one labeled "More." If they are a second-degree Connection to you, you will see the "Connect" button and the "More" button. Click on "More" and you'll see a number of interesting options. One is "Share Profile."

Click on it and you will be walked through the introduction and how to share the Profiles.

I've noticed that LinkedIn lists "People who viewed my Profile Also Viewed." Is that a useful list?

Yes, there are two ways this list can help you. The first is that if you see second-degree Connections on that list, they might already know you or of you and could be good people to invite as Connections. The second is that the list gives you some useful feedback about what people believe they know about you. For example, if you have a focused area of practice and the list indicates people from an old practice area or a more general practice, you have some good feedback that it might be time to emphasize your specific area of practice.

Can I disconnect from a Connection or block someone from viewing my Profile?

LinkedIn provides a full and complete (and probably comforting) answer at *https://www.linkedin.com/help/linkedin/answer/2839*. The short answer is yes. Only you can unblock them and, as a general matter, they will not be notified that you blocked them. Remember that you can also adjust your Profile settings to limit what information about you (such as email or phone numbers) get shared. You can also choose only to display a last initial and not to have a photo. You can remove a first-degree Connection either by (1) going to their Profile page, clicking on the "More" button, and choosing "Remove Connection" or (2) going to your Connections list, finding them, clicking on the "More" button, and choosing "Remove Connection." It is worth noting that when you remove a connection, they won't be notified and any recommendations or endorsements between you and that person will be withdrawn. (We talk more about blocking and unfollowing in Chapter 17)

Should I prevent other people from seeing my Connections or Profile?

You can keep search engines or non-members of LinkedIn from seeing your public Profile by going to your Profile, clicking the "Edit public profile & URL" in the right column and toggling "Your profile's public visibility" to Off. Strategically, we are not sure that it ever makes sense to hide your Connections from others, but if you choose to, you can make them visible only to your first-degree Connections or just to yourself. Go to your privacy settings. Under the "How others see your profile and network information" you will see a choice labeled "Who can see your connections." Select your preferred visibility setting.

If I receive an invitation to connect, do I have to accept it?

No. You can click to delete it or keep it in your inbox to make a decision about it later. Don't feel any pressure—it's your choice. Remember that choosing to "follow" that person rather than add them as a Connection is another approach to take. You can also change your mind and remove that person as a Connection later. Take whatever approach feels most comfortable to you—connecting is a mutual process.

Should I buy LinkedIn Connections?

Amazingly, there is a market for selling you LinkedIn Connections. Google "buying LinkedIn Connections." We cannot imagine any scenario or strategy for a legal professional where buying Connections makes sense. In fact, we see many ways it could backfire. However, there do seem to be sellers of blocks of Connections. What kind of network would that give you? We've seen prices of $50 for 500 Connections—what could possibly go wrong? Seriously, though, we would never advise this approach.

PART IV

PARTICIPATION

15

PARTICIPATING ON LINKEDIN: POSTS AND GROUPS

P articipation is the third essential LinkedIn building block, and the one that is the most often overlooked or neglected. A robust, up-to-date Profile is necessary so that LinkedIn users can decide whether they want to connect or engage with you. Your Connections are important for you to establish relationships and gain visibility. Participation is what is going to help you to engage with others and make those relationships work for you. Most people who complain that they have not seen the results they want from LinkedIn have done a poor job in the area of Participation.

Remember, LinkedIn is, first and foremost, a networking and relationship-building platform, not a sales platform. The essence of networking is participation. The true value of networking is building and strengthening real, genuine relationships with people on the network who are in your target audience—or who can get you to your target audience—whether that target audience is potential clients, referral sources, or strategic alliances.

Think about how you network in real life: having a good-looking business card, joining organizations, attending events, and exchanging contact information is not enough on its own to establish real, long-lasting relationships.

To get real traction in any organization, and to establish deeper relationships, you need to do more than just be a member. You need to participate. In real life, that may mean joining a committee, volunteering to help at an event, etc. The same is true on LinkedIn.

The real value comes from engagement and interaction, not just from collecting Connections. Whether you are already connected to your target audience or not, you need to nurture relationships and be an active participant to get the full benefit of LinkedIn. The chapters in this section will show you how.

Conventional marketing wisdom says it usually takes anywhere from seven to twelve "touches" before someone will do business with you. Those touches can include e-mail, in-person contacts, advertisements, direct referrals, articles, and the like. Even after someone does business with you or refers a client for the first time, however, you must continue your efforts to remain memorable so that he or she will keep working with you. Sharing Posts and participating in Groups on LinkedIn are great ways to communicate with your network on an ongoing basis and keep your name at the forefront of your target audience.

Let's begin with Posts (formerly called Updates).

Posts

If all you're doing is consuming others' content on LinkedIn and not creating your own content, you're missing a huge opportunity. Creating content makes you more visible on LinkedIn because it gets you in front of your network in their Feed. This drives engagement, which also drives connections and followers. After all, why would someone follow or engage with you on LinkedIn if you don't participate and there's nothing there to engage with?

Posts are short messages, similar to Facebook posts or Twitter tweets. You share Posts with your network directly from the top of your LinkedIn Home page by clicking on "Start a post."

Stay professional and stay on-topic for business; LinkedIn is the "professional network"—posts about your vacations, pets, and last night's dinner are more appropriate for a social network like Facebook or Instagram. As an experiment, Dennis recently posted a photo from a concert he attended and was asked why he posted something personal and whether he should be doing that. On the other hand, quite a few people viewed, liked and commented on the post, including people who were fans of the artist. You might experiment. As a general matter, however, be very wary about posting political content, especially in an election year. You are likely to hear that you should "post that stuff on Facebook." A good guideline is to think about whether you would be comfortable sharing the content of your Post in a conversation with a client, colleague or referral source; if so, feel free to post it.

Do not be too self-promotional. We recommend that your LinkedIn Posts be 80% informational and 20% promotional. But even "promotional" Posts should provide value in some way to your network. For example, a link to an article, blog post, or presentation is self-promotional in one sense, but it also links the reader to content that might be useful. Think about what you like and don't like to see in Posts from your Connections. Monitor the number of views and likes your Posts to help you determine what kinds of Posts work best with your audience.

LinkedIn gives you several options for sharing your Posts. To show the Post to everyone in your extended network, including all degrees of your Connections, as well as to others, select "Anyone". To show the Post only to your first-degree connections, select "Connections". To show your Post to both LinkedIn and Twitter, select "Anyone + Twitter". Once you join some Groups on LinkedIn, you will also see a list of your Groups in the drop-down menu, which allows you to easily share a post with your LinkedIn Groups directly from your Home page.

LinkedIn Posts have a larger character limit (up to 1300 characters) than Twitter's character limit, although if you plan to cross-post from LinkedIn to Twitter, you might want to stick with a post that will fit within the shorter limit. Also, if you post a link longer than 26 characters, LinkedIn will automatically shorten it for you. On desktop, only the first 210 characters will be shown of your post before the "see more" link.

What to Include in a LinkedIn Post

When creating any Post on LinkedIn, even posts that are about you or your practice, keep your audience in mind. Use the "So what?" test when composing Posts: Ask yourself why your network would care about what you have to say. Think about how it relates to them and their businesses. Are your Posts informative and/or entertaining? Do they provide value for your audience? Observe carefully what others in your network do well and consider whether to adopt a similar approach—are their Posts getting noticed? Do they provoke engagement in the form of comments, likes or shares?

Creating content for LinkedIn doesn't have to be a time or labor-intensive process. Re-purpose what you already have. For example, take the first few paragraphs or a few key take-aways from an article you've written for your website or for another publication and post them as an article on LinkedIn (you can post a link to the full article at the end, driving traffic to your site); pull quotes from your articles and post text updates; share images from your firm's events; post links to articles written by others with your own commentary; or share slides of your most recent presentation.

Here are some ideas for effective LinkedIn Posts:

► If you have your own blog, provide the title of a recent post with a shortened URL link (from TinyURL or Bit.ly) to reduce the number of characters in the Post.

- Link to an article you read that might be of interest to your network, especially if it relates to your practice area, local community, or your clients' industries.

- Post a brief note about a recent court decision, new regulation, or news story relevant to your area of practice.

- Link to a short YouTube video that can provide value to your network.

- Mention an important announcement or news item about you or your firm (this also can be a great cross-selling tool).

- Link to an article in which you are quoted; include the publication, article title, and a short description (if space allows).

- Link to an event or industry conference you are attending (or simply include the fact of your attendance).

- Post an interesting fact or tip you learned from attending a conference, presentation or lecture.

- Announce a presentation you are giving and/or provide a link to a copy of your slides after a presentation (this is especially effective if you've uploaded your presentation to LinkedIn SlideShare).

- Link to resources that might be useful to your audience.

- Try to add a photo or link to a page that generates a photo in the post for you; posts with images tend to get noticed more easily, which translates into increased engagement.

- Ask a question to create discussion with your Connections.

If your Posts provide value to others, they can be powerful PR and brand-building tools. Your network will begin to look to you and your Posts as a valuable source of information, in turn building your expert status.

Your LinkedIn posts appear on the Home page of each of your Connections, in their Feed. But, as with other platforms, your post most likely will not be visible for long in the Feed, given the volume of activity on LinkedIn, especially if your Connection has several other Connections posting frequent Posts. That is another reason you want to make sure that your Posts provide value to your Network. LinkedIn sorts the Feed by "Top" posts, not reverse chronological order. In other words, the more engagement a Post gets, the more likely it is that it will show in the Feeds of your Connections. And, thinking back to the feedback loop we discussed in Chapter 4, the more engagement a Post receives, the more value you're bringing to your Network.

Connections can also view your Posts and other activity on your Profile in the Articles and Activity section that appears above Experience if they want to see more of what you are sharing.

Making your Posts memorable and useful will help your Posts to rise to the top, but even popular Posts will not be seen by every one of your Connections, so don't worry too much about annoying your Connections with frequent posts. In fact, most legal professionals post far too infrequently to make any impact.

Networking is not a one-way street; when you receive Posts by e-mail or on your LinkedIn Home page, pay attention. Take note of what others in your Network are talking about. Occasionally send notes in response via InMail, e-mail, or regular mail or make a phone call. We'll talk more about engaging with your Network in Chapter 17.

Groups

One of the best ways to build stronger relationships within LinkedIn is through Groups. There are LinkedIn Groups organized around almost any topic you can think of: alumni, industries, practice areas, hobbies, and many more. If you cannot find a Group to suit your needs or interests, you can start your own. Find the Groups under the "Work" tab to the extreme right of the navigation bar on the desktop version, or by looking to the left of your Feed on the Home page. You can also find your Groups listed under your photo on the top of the app to the left of the search bar.

Finding Groups to Join

Search Groups for your target market, your industry, your clients' industries, your practice area, or your alma mater. To make it even easier, search for Groups to which you already belong in the real world. Many bar associations, lawyers' groups, and community groups have corresponding LinkedIn Groups.

Choose Groups that are big enough to have depth but small enough to allow you to be visible and to actively contribute.

Some Groups will allow you to join immediately, whereas others are moderated, and you must "apply" to be accepted. Groups are moderated to ensure that the messages and participation will not include spam and that a prospective member is someone who legitimately should be part of the Group.

To get the most benefit from Groups, you must be an active participant—that means discussing, writing, commenting, and connecting with Group members. When you participate, other members will see your picture, name, and professional headline, and from there they can click to see your full Profile or to send you a message.

What to Do in Groups

We suggest that you choose a few Groups that especially appeal to you and in which you likely will become active. Avoid spreading yourself too thin; this can lead to "Group overload" and may impede participation. Although you can join several Groups, the better approach is to first simply monitor them to see if they are what you think they are and if they actually interest you before actively participating.

Begin by viewing others' Posts in the Group and contributing where you can add value. You can view the Group Posts by going to that Group's Page and scrolling down the Feed, similar to the Feed on your Home page, but limited to posts within that specific Group.

An easy way to get started participating in Groups is to "like" or comment on a post or discussion started by another Group member by clicking on the Like or Comment buttons at the bottom of a posting or to share it with your network. This is part of the "karma" of LinkedIn (and of all good networking)—give before you receive. Sharing others' work brings them visibility; eventually, it will come back to you. People will seek out opportunities to reciprocate.

Once you get a feel for the Group culture, you can begin posting your own discussions, which may include linking back to content on your website or blog. Be sure the content you post and to which you link is appropriate for the Group and is not just a sales pitch; read each Group's rules carefully. When linking to articles of interest not authored by you, we recommend that instead of just posting the link, you add your own commentary, ask a question, or make a statement to encourage interaction. The big idea: add value to Groups whenever you can. Be a giver, not just a taker.

The Benefits of Groups

In Groups, people share information, brainstorm ideas, discuss their interests and challenges, post informational articles or links, and conduct polls, making it easy for you to get to know others and for them to get to know you.

Groups can provide fodder for your other online activities—for example, blog posts and tweets—to create a fully integrated online marketing presence. Get ideas from Groups containing your target market about what they are interested in, what their concerns are, and what services might be helpful to them just by watching the discussion.

When you join a Group, you can see the list of members, making it easy to identify people with particular interests or challenges and to navigate to their Profiles for more information. You will also see who the influencers are—those who participate regularly, whose advice others seek, and who provide great answers or provoke interesting discussions.

Another advantage to belonging to Groups is that you can easily add other Group members as Connections. Simply go to the Group homepage and find the Group member you want to invite. Click on the link for that member and you'll go to their Profile and be able to send an invitation. In addition, you can send other Group members who are Connections up to fifteen 1:1 messages a month. However, once you are connected to another Group member, it is much easier to communicate with that person directly.

Active participation in Groups helps you become known as a subject matter expert. Your Posts to your network can establish you as someone who shares valuable content, but Groups takes that one step further. In Group discussions you have more "real estate" to demonstrate your knowledge and provide real help and information-packed content. And best of all, when you participate in Group discussions, you reach beyond your Connections list.

Start Your Own Group

Although it is a good idea to get involved in an existing Group, especially when starting out on LinkedIn, there are good reasons for starting your own Group (if you are up to it). It can be difficult to get a new Group started and, especially, to keep it going, but if you think you have something different to offer, you might try to start your own Group and see how successful it can be. For example, we started the Group "Social Networking for Lawyers" quite a few years ago. Our experience has been a rocky one, to say the least. We're not sure it's even fair to call it an "active" Group at this point. Building and sustaining a Group over the long haul is a challenging task.

You must do a lot of work up front to get a Group going. Our advice is to focus on bringing people together who can benefit from sharing mutual experiences and insights. Start some discussions. Invite your Connections to join the Group. Ask other Group members to participate by starting discussions or joining in on existing ones. Tap other Group members to be Managers to help share the load.

Just because there is one Group on a particular subject does not mean that there cannot be others on the same subject. However, you will want to see what is going on in the other Groups first and determine whether it makes sense to join them or to create your own space with your own audience. You might create a Group with a local focus or a narrow or specific topic to carve out your own space. It really comes down to answering the question "What do you want?"

It is easy to underestimate how much time and effort it might take to promote your Group and get it to a point of critical mass. As a Group owner, you get a lot of helpful management tools for approving members, moderating conversations, and much more, but managing a Group will require a time commitment and regular management chores. As an owner, you will probably need to seed discussions and have a regular presence in the Group to engage others.

Posts and Groups are just two of the participation tools available on LinkedIn. For more ways to participate, let us move to Chapter 16, where we discuss Endorsements and Recommendations.

16

SOCIAL PROOF: ENDORSEMENTS AND RECOMMENDATIONS

Active LinkedIn users take advantage of two other powerful techniques to enhance their reputation and increase not only the value they provide to their networks but also the value of their networks to their Connections. These techniques are Endorsements and Recommendations, and they work on LinkedIn much as they do in the real world—as third-party proof or, as some say, "social proof." It is an opportunity for those who view your Profile to see what others say about you, not just what you say about yourself.

LinkedIn Endorsements

LinkedIn introduced Endorsements in 2013, with a heavy promotional effort and a prominent placement on Profile pages. LinkedIn claims that more than one billion endorsements were given in first half of 2013 alone. However, in more recent years, it appears that LinkedIn has backed off of Endorsements significantly. For example, LinkedIn no longer allows Connections to suggest Endorsements for you. Endorsements can only be given for Skills already listed on your Profile. And, although LinkedIn presents users with the opportunity to provide Endorsements when viewing a Connection's Profile, it is not as aggressive in doing so as it used to be (at least in our opinion).

Endorsements are a simple one-click way for your Connections to vouch for your expertise in a particular area or for you to do the same for your Connections. Endorsements are tied to the specific Skills on your Profile. You can think of them as a lightweight form of recommendation, similar in many ways to the idea of "liking" someone's comment or Post. You don't need to write a detailed recommendation; all you do is click on a specific Skill to show that you endorse your Connection for that Skill. You do need to be mindful of which Skills you receive Endorsements for and what you endorse others for, as you'll see below.

Now when you endorse a Connection for a Skill on their Profile, LinkedIn may display a pop-up box asking you for additional information; whether you connection is "good, very good, or highly skilled" at that particular Skill, and how you know about their ability—what your relationship with that connection is (you worked on the project with them, supervised them, worked for them, or heard about the skill from others). You might also be asked to answer other questions, including who you would go to for questions about a particular Skill. It is unclear as of now how LinkedIn is or intends to use this information, but for the time being, it is not shared with your Connections.

If you have Skills listed on your Profile (and you definitely should if it is not prohibited under the ethical rules for your jurisdiction), you may receive an e-mail from LinkedIn notifying you that someone has endorsed you for a Skill. Click on the blue "Review Endorsements" button in the e-mail, which will take you to your LinkedIn account to review the Endorsement and determine whether you would like to keep it on your Profile.

You may also be notified of new Endorsements through the Notifications tab on both the LinkedIn mobile app and the desktop version of LinkedIn. You can turn off Endorsement Notifications for both the mobile app and/or the desktop site through your Settings.

Endorsements are shown on your Profile in the Skills and Endorsements section. LinkedIn users will initially see up to three "featured" Skills, but if you have more than three Skills on your Profile, users can click on "See more" to see the remainder of your Skills. A number next to each Skill indicates how many Endorsements you have received for that Skill. Clicking on the number next to the Skill will reveal the list of names and photographs of those who have Endorsed you for that Skill.

As noted above, in the past, LinkedIn allowed Connections to suggest a new Skills to be added to your Profile. This may have resulted in Skills being added to your Profile that you no longer possess (or never even had). Although LinkedIn has now eliminated that ability, we recommend that all LinkedIn users review the Skills listed on their Profile to ensure that they are accurate and up to date.

If you are uncomfortable with a particular Endorsement on your Profile, you can delete it. Go to the Skills & Endorsements section and click on the pencil icon to edit that section. Here you can add or remove Skills, change the display settings for Endorsements, and change your settings to choose whether you want to be endorsed, whether you want to see endorsement suggestions for your connections, or to re-order your Skills.

If you want to remove an Endorsement from a Skill, click on that Skill itself, which will provide you with a list of those who have endorsed you; you can then choose to make that Endorsement invisible.

If you do not wish to receive Endorsements from your Connections, you can choose to opt out of receiving Endorsements by clicking the edit icon and then selecting "Adjust Endorsement Settings" at the bottom.

Endorsing Others for Skills on Their Profile

One rule of thumb we recommend is to only endorse people you know well for Skills you have personally observed.

You can also un-endorse someone for whom you made an Endorsement if you later change your mind. To do so, go to the Skills section of that Connection's Profile, and find the Skill you endorsed them for. You will see a check mark next to that Skill (instead of the plus sign); click the check mark to remove the Endorsement.

LinkedIn likes Endorsements because they are a way to show directly on your Profile what you're actually good at, not because *you* say you are, but because others agree you are. Over time, if you have a LinkedIn Profile with Skills listed and no one has endorsed you for those Skills, it will call your expertise into question, particularly if you have a significant number of Connections. However, you need to monitor Endorsements closely and be aware of potential ethical concerns, which we will discuss in Chapter 28.

Recommendations

Recommendations are just what you would expect: a way for clients, colleagues, employers, coworkers, referral sources, and strategic alliances to recommend your work or for you to recommend theirs. Recommendations are like reference letters that appear on a LinkedIn Profile, which might raise issues about testimonials or endorsements under ethical rules. Compared with Endorsements, Recommendations are often more thoughtful, well-written, and well-considered mini essays about work you've done, how much people like working with you, and similar topics.

Recommendations are useful for all of the same reasons that reference letters and testimonials are useful. What a third party says about you is always more valuable than what you say about yourself. Recommendations can highlight specific aspects of your service or tell a story about what it is like to work with you. And, according to LinkedIn, users with Recommendations are three times as likely to get inquiries through LinkedIn searches as those with no Recommendations.

Recommendations you receive are listed in the Recommendations section of your Profile, which appears below Skills and Endorsements. This section of your Profile shows both the Recommendations you have received and the Recommendations you have given, although the default view is received Recommendations.

Click the pencil icon within that section to manage both Recommendations you have received and those you have given. Here, you can determine whether to make a Recommendation visible or to request a revision.

If you want to request a Recommendation, click "Ask for a Recommendation" to the left of the pencil icon in the Recommendations section. This will bring up a series of questions for you to answer to help your Connection make the Recommendation. Then enter the name of the Connection from whom you are requesting the Recommendation and create your request message. You can also request a Recommendation from a Connection's Profile by clicking on the More button in the introduction card and then clicking on Request a recommendation.

You may only request Recommendations for Experience or Education. If you'd like to request a Recommendation for volunteer work, you'll have to create a separate entry for it under Experience.

Requesting a Revision of a Recommendation

One of the things that makes Recommendations valuable is that only the person writing the Recommendation has control over the content of the Recommendation. As the owner of the Profile on which the Recommendation is posted, you have only three options for Recommendations you receive: post the recommendation as written, hide the post from your Profile, or request a revision of the Recommendation from the person who provided it.

There are occasions when you may wish to request a revision of a Recommendation you have received on LinkedIn. Some examples might include a Recommendation received from a client which contains prohibited language (See Chapter 28 on ethics), or a Recommendation that includes a typographical error or factual error.

You can request a revision of a Recommendation by clicking on the individual recommendation and then clicking on "request a revision." In the mobile app, navigate to the Recommendations section, click the pencil icon, and then click the pencil icon again in the top right corner. Now you will see the options under each recommendation to show or hide, or to request a revision.

Recommendation Request Tips

- ► Do not rely on the stock message created by LinkedIn.

- ► Customize the request for each recipient.

- ► Ask for a Recommendation on a specific project or request that your Connection discuss a specific aspect of your service, your approach, or your Skills to make Recommendations useful and varied and help paint a well-rounded picture of who you are and why people like you.

- ▶ When you receive a nice compliment from any of your Connections outside of LinkedIn, ask them if they would mind posting their comments as a Recommendation on LinkedIn and send them a request.

- ▶ If you are concerned about receiving Recommendations from clients, ask for Recommendations from referral sources, colleagues, coworkers, or others who are familiar with your work.

- ▶ Request Recommendations from organizations where you are active: charitable boards, local bar associations, volunteer or community groups, etc.

- ▶ Review and approve Recommendations from your Connections; make and request revisions where necessary.

Recommending Others

Writing a Recommendation for another professional (even if you haven't been asked to do so) is a good way to express your appreciation for a job well done or to give back. To make a Recommendation, navigate to the Recommendations section on their Profile and click on the box that says "Recommend [Connection name]". You can also click the "more" button at the top of their Profile in the Introduction Card and click on Recommend.

Once your Recommendation has been completed, LinkedIn will notify the recipient, who will be asked to approve or reject it. LinkedIn allows only approved Recommendations to appear on a user's Profile and gives the option to show or hide Recommendations. The recipient can also request revisions to a Recommendation, as mentioned above.

It's good to revisit the Recommendations that display on your Profile from time to time and consider removing old ones that do not relate to what you are doing now.

Now that you are participating more actively on LinkedIn, learn how you can monitor your activity and the activity of those in your network in Chapter 17.

17

MONITORING AND ENGAGING WITH YOUR NETWORK

As we have said before, in many ways, LinkedIn is an extension of your real-world network, and the same principles of networking apply. LinkedIn makes it easy for you to do what the best real-world networkers work very hard to accomplish: consistently monitoring and engaging with their network.

Great real-world networkers have an uncanny ability to know what is happening in their networks. They seem to know who moved to another firm before anyone else does, who is looking for a new job, who has won an award, and other news. They also know who in their network is working with someone else in the network (perhaps because they facilitated that engagement) and who should be meeting someone else. In other words, they have a great sense of community.

For these people, obtaining this information seems effortless and second nature. The rest of us wonder how they find any time to work given how much time they must spend keeping up with goings-on in their networks.

LinkedIn gives us tools to monitor what is happening in our networks in simple yet comprehensive ways so that we each can have the kind of "eyes and ears" that the best real-world networkers have. In fact, using LinkedIn, you can keep up with your network in just a few minutes daily or weekly.

Your LinkedIn Feed

When you log in to your LinkedIn account, your LinkedIn Home page appears. The Home page includes many elements and provides several features and sources of information about your LinkedIn world, but the main element you see on your Home page is your Feed in the middle of the page, directly below the post box. You can also interact with your Network on the Home page (the house icon) in the app.

The Feed is similar to your Facebook feed—it contains the posts from your Network and people you follow, along with some ads, sponsored posts, and posts that people in your network have interacted with.

By default, LinkedIn organizes the Feed by placing the content LinkedIn deems to be the "Top" posts (usually those that have received a lot of engagement) at the top of the feed, but on the desktop version you can change that by clicking on the down arrow at the top of the Feed where it says, "Sort by" and choose "Recent" instead, if you would like to see posts in reverse chronological order, with the newest posts at the top of the Feed. As of the time this book was published, you do not have the option to display your Feed in reverse chronological order in the mobile app. Note that some of the features described below might work differently in the app or might not yet be fully implemented.

You can also improve your Feed by clicking on the three dots at the top right of any Post in your Feed (on the desktop version) or by clicking on the down arrow at the top right of the post (on the mobile app) and click on "Improve my Feed" to get recommendations for Influencers, hashtags, Companies and other sources of information to follow.

Recently, we've noticed that LinkedIn is putting a lot of emphasis on hashtags, suggesting hashtags to you at the bottom of your posts and encouraging users to discover and follow hashtags. On the left side of your Home page, next to your Feed, you'll find the hashtags you follow and the link to discover more. On the mobile app, click on the thumbnail of your profile photo with the three lines in a circle in the top left corner of the app to open a panel where you can see the hashtags you follow and find additional ones.

The Feed gives you one convenient place within which to monitor what people in your Network are talking about. Spending a few minutes each day or a few times a week there will level the playing field with the best real-world networkers. But it can also provide you with insights and content to share with your network.

Notifications

Another way to monitor your Network on LinkedIn is through Notifications which you can find in the navigation bar at the top of every page in LinkedIn in the desktop version and through emails sent by LinkedIn, depending on your communications settings (we talk about settings in Chapter 3). On the mobile app, you can find notifications by clicking on the bell icon at the bottom of the screen.

Common notifications include:

► Connection invitations received

► Endorsements received

► Profile views

► Post mentions

► Comments or shares of your posts

► Daily summaries or "rundowns" of news

► Articles published by your Connections

► Birthdays or work anniversaries of your Connections

Liking, Sharing, Commenting and Tagging

At the heart of networking is building relationships. It isn't enough to just show up or "lurk" and watch what other people are doing. You have to participate and engage with the people in your network. Sometimes that means creating your own content or sharing content you think your audience will find valuable, as we discuss in Chapter 18. But there are even easier (and faster) ways to engage on LinkedIn by using LinkedIn's social features: liking, sharing, commenting and tagging.

Below each post, whether you see it in your Feed or in a Group discussion on the desktop or in the app, is a "**Like**" button. Hovering over this button on desktop or holding it on the mobile app allows you to choose from several reactions to a post: like, celebrate, love, insightful or curious. In the legal realm, it's safe to assume that most will stick with the simple "like" for the foreseeable future on most posts, although we are seeing a bit more variety as users get more familiar with these different reactions. Choosing to react to a post lets the people in your Network or who you follow know that you are interested in what they are sharing, and that you are paying attention. Your likes will also show up in your Activity on your Profile, so others can see what kind of content you engage with.

People in the network of the person who originally posted the content can also see who has reacted to the post. And reacting to a post on LinkedIn helps boost that post's visibility in the Feed—the more engagement, the more that post will show up at the top of the Feeds of people who follow the person who posted it.

Commenting on a post takes things one step further than just reacting—and many LinkedIn users will choose to both react and comment to the same post. Taking the time to write a comment shows a deeper level of engagement with your Connection. It provides an opportunity for discussion not only with the person who created the post, but with others in your connection's network who might also see the post.

Comments boost the post's visibility, and your visibility, both inside and outside of your Network. Creating a comment also may make the post show up in the Feeds of people in your Network as a result of your engagement with the post. You may have seen posts in your Feed from people you do not follow and are not connected to on LinkedIn, with a message at the top like "Dennis Kennedy commented on this." Writing a comment is yet another opportunity to demonstrate your expertise or to develop relationships through LinkedIn, both inside and outside of your network.

Sharing a post is another great way to not only provide value to your network through the Feed, but it also helps boost visibility for the post and for your Connection who made it. If you are short on time or are having difficulty thinking of topics to post about, Sharing is a good way to stay engaged with your Network with minimal effort. Simply scroll through your Feed on LinkedIn and hit the "Share" button at the bottom of posts that would be of interest to your Connections.

Tagging people in LinkedIn posts is another little-used but very effective technique for getting more engagement with your network. You tag someone by typing the @ symbol and then starting to type their first or last name. As you type, a list of suggested names will drop down. Choose the one you want and the tagged name will be inserted for you and appear in bold.

When you tag someone in a post, they get a special notification about the post. Most people, when they are tagged in a post, will naturally want to read the post to find out why they have been tagged. Frequently, the tagged people will leave a comment, share or react to the post, once again, creating that all-important engagement and expanding the reach of your post. Tagging is a great tactic when you post about someone's article or other content.

When you have been tagged in a post, you will also then receive notifications about engagement with that post, just as you would if you had made the post yourself.

In 2019, LinkedIn also added the ability to tag people in photos, the way you can tag them on Facebook.

Messaging on LinkedIn

Messaging is the way you speak to others one on one in LinkedIn. In 2019, LinkedIn even added the ability to send a video message through the platform. You can find your sent and received Messages on the Messages tab, with the quote bubble icon in both the desktop site and on the mobile app. It appears in the main navigation bar in the desktop version, and at the upper right corner on the mobile app. When on the desktop site, you'll also see the Messages tab at the lower right corner, which enables you to see Messages in real time.

Sending individual Messages through LinkedIn can be a powerful way to engage with your Connections on a deeper level, and an important step in building relationships with your Connections. Just like in real life, conversing in public (such as in Comment threads on LinkedIn) or at events (joining Group discussion on LinkedIn) with several people at a time can be helpful for getting the attention of your Connections and their Followers and Connections, but building real relationships requires one-on-one contact. Messages are a good way to start these one-on-one conversations (which hopefully you'll then take offline, too).

Be aware that many people do not check LinkedIn messages on a regular basis, so do not expect "instant" replies. Often, after the first message or two, people will switch over to email. LinkedIn messaging is a good tool when you are connected to someone but do not have their current email address or phone number handy. On the other hand, you might find that LinkedIn messaging becomes the primary way that you communicate with some of your LinkedIn Connections.

When you send some (but not all) messages through LinkedIn, such as an InMail message or a connection request with a message, like an email message, it will contain both a subject and a body. Give some thought to your subject line—it might make or break your message. If the subject line doesn't capture the attention of the person you are sending the message to, they may not ever get to the body of the message. Keep both your subject line and the body of your message short and sweet; your goal is to start or continue a conversation with this LinkedIn user. Try to be as concise as possible.

As of the time of publication of this book, whether on the desktop version or the mobile app, LinkedIn does not provide a place to add a subject line to regular Messages to your Connections.

One of the benefits of joining Groups on LinkedIn is that you have access to Group members who might be 3rd level or higher connections through the Group. You can send individual Messages to Group members by navigating to the Group, clicking on "see all" to get a list of the members, and then clicking on "Message" next to the member's name. Regardless of how remote the connection is, you will be able to contact them directly, up to a limit (currently you can send up to 15 of these kinds of messages per month).

Benefits of Monitoring and Engaging with Your Network

LinkedIn tools automatically and conveniently bring you information supplied by those in your network through your Feed and your

Notifications. You can leverage that information much more quickly and easily through LinkedIn than you often would be able to otherwise. For example, imagine that one of your contacts gets a new job. You may or may not hear of their change of circumstance or have their new contact information. But with LinkedIn you automatically receive a notice of the change in real time because the contact changed his or her LinkedIn Profile. This will allow you to not only congratulate them on LinkedIn, which LinkedIn makes extraordinarily easy to do by suggesting some simple pre-written messages, but to take steps in the real world to deepen your relationship by sending a card, calling the contact with your congratulations or asking how the new job is going the next time you see that person. Turning LinkedIn information into real-world actions is the key to realizing the most value from your use of LinkedIn.

Monitoring your network should be a regular, ongoing process, and it has never been easier than it is with LinkedIn. In many ways, LinkedIn does all the work for you. All you need to do then is to take action on the information you receive.

Following Companies and Organizations

Another way to obtain intelligence from LinkedIn is by following companies or organizations on LinkedIn. Many companies have established Company Pages on the platform. A Company Page on LinkedIn represents a business or organization, rather than an individual. Individuals create Profiles, and companies create Pages on LinkedIn. We discuss Company Pages in more detail in Chapter 26.

There are several different ways that you can find and follow Company Pages. You can search for Companies on LinkedIn using the search box in the navigation bar. Or, when viewing a Connection's Profile, you may see a company logo next to entries in the

Experience section. If a logo appears on LinkedIn, it means that business or organization has a LinkedIn Company Page. Click on the logo and you will be taken to the Company Page, where you can click the Follow button to add that business' posts to your Feed. Most colleges and universities also have Pages on LinkedIn.

Recently we've noticed that when someone accepts your invitation to connect, or you accept their invitation, LinkedIn will suggest that you follow their current business' Company Page (if it exists).

Why Find and Follow Company Pages?

Company Pages can provide insight into a client or colleague's business interests, or simply help you keep up with what is happening in a particular organization or industry. In addition, one of the most useful things we've found about Company Pages is that you can see who is employed at the Company that has a LinkedIn Profile. This can be incredibly useful at identifying Connections within a business or industry you are targeting—possibly for introductions—and also for finding the person or persons that have a specific title or job description within a business or industry—information which is rarely easily obtainable elsewhere.

Blocking users, reporting bad behavior and withdrawing invitations

We hate to say it, but just like in real life, occasionally you will encounter people on LinkedIn who engage in bad behavior, send spam messages, are too focused on selling rather than building relationships, and more. As a result, you may find that you want to disengage from those people on LinkedIn and/or to block them from seeing what you do on the platform. You can also proactively block users. For example, if you have difficulty with someone in the real world, you can proactively block them from seeing your activity on LinkedIn before they attempt to connect with you.

If you have already connected to someone and are now regretting it, disconnect by navigating to the Profile of the person you want to block and click on "More" in the introduction card at the top of their Profile. Scroll down and choose "block or report" and then "Continue."

You'll be taken to another screen to confirm that you want to block this person. Once you have completed the blocking process, that LinkedIn user will appear on your blocked list, which you can find under the Profile tab of your Settings, under Privacy Controls; you'll see a link entitled, "Manage who you're blocking." You can unblock them later if you choose to do so, but you'll have to send a new invitation to connect if you'd like to be connected, and you won't be able to re-block that person for 48 hours.

Once you have blocked someone on LinkedIn, that person will no longer see you in their Who's Viewed Your Profile section, and they will not be notified that you have blocked them. That member will no longer have access to your Profile and will not be able to message you through LinkedIn. They won't see your Posts, and any Recommendations or Endorsements you received from them will disappear from your Profile.

Similarly, when you've blocked someone, you will no longer be able to view their Profile or their Posts or send them messages through LinkedIn. However, both you and the blocked user will still have access to information each of you has shared publicly such as your Public Profile, or content posted in Group discussions in which you are both members.

If blocking is too extreme a remedy for you, but you simply no longer want to be connected to someone on LinkedIn, instead of clicking on "block or report" under "More" on their Profile, click "Unfollow." Or, go to your "My Network" page, find that connection in your list, and click on the three dots in the right column and then click on "Remove Connection."

If you sent an invitation to connect and it hasn't yet been accepted, you may withdraw the invitation if you wish. To do so, go to your "My Network" page, click on "See All" at the top of the page, and then click "Sent". Click on "Withdraw" next to the invitation you want to withdraw. If you mistakenly sent invitations to your entire address book when you imported your contacts into LinkedIn, you can withdraw those invitations by clicking on "contacts imported from your address book" and then clicking withdraw. Keep in mind that once you withdraw a sent invitation, LinkedIn will not allow you to send that person another invitation for three weeks.

There are also some indications that LinkedIn will limit your ability to send additional invitations if you send too many. We've noticed that it appears that your "People You May Know" list might not change as quickly if you have sent a lot of invitations recently or have a large number of pending invitations. Realistically, if someone has not accepted your invitation in a few weeks, the odds that they will are quite small, although there are some users who will log in to LinkedIn rarely and accept invitations that are quite old. One approach is to go ahead and withdraw the invitation to reduce the size of your outstanding invitations list and, if you would still like to be connected with them, wait a while (at least three weeks) and send a new invitation later.

If you're receiving invitations to connect on LinkedIn that are clearly spam, for example an invitation with an advertisement, you can report it as spam by clicking "Ignore" and then "Report as Spam," which notifies LinkedIn that the message is a problem. Other signs to watch for include the inviter has a very small number of Connections, zero or just a few common Connections with you, has a minimally completed Profile, a photo that looks more like a swimsuit model than an accountant, and the like.

When you receive unwanted messages, report them to LinkedIn. You can report the message by clicking on the three dots at the upper right corner of the message and clicking "report."

Don't let LinkedIn users who are abusing the platform ruin your LinkedIn experience. Manage your Connections and remember to use caution when accepting invitations to connect.

You can also help reduce LinkedIn spam by appropriately using your Settings. You can restrict who can send you invitations to connect through LinkedIn only to those people who have your email address or whose contacts you have imported yourself. If you decide to do this, make sure you keep your imported contacts address book updated. And check the Blocked Messages in your LinkedIn Inbox (go to your inbox, click on all messages, then blocked messages) to review messages blocked so that you don't miss an important invitation. (We discussed more privacy and security settings in Chapter 3.)

Blocking and Groups

If you're the manager of a Group and you want to block someone who is a Group member, you'll need to remove them from the Group before you can block them, and if the person you want to block is the manager of a Group that you are a member of, you will need to leave the Group before you can block them.

In Groups, owners or managers can remove or block any member by using the "Manage" tab within the Group. Removing a member takes the member out of the Group but does not delete past contributions, and the member can request to join again. Blocking members will prevent them from joining again, but their past contributions still will not be removed. However, Group owners and managers have the ability to remove conversations or specific comments from a Group individually by navigating to that conversation or comment, clicking on the More icon, and selecting the delete option. Regular Group members can remove their own conversations or comments but cannot delete conversations or comments contributed by other Group members.

Group members can see every individual member's contributions, and you can't prevent other Group members from following you unless you leave the Group. LinkedIn also makes it easier for Group members to request invitations to connect. You can combat that by making your invitation requirements stricter, but this might affect your own attempts to try to connect with other people as well.

As you can see, LinkedIn provides many different tools to help you monitor and engage with your network or with individuals or businesses outside of your network that you would like to get to know, or to develop relationships with. Some of these tools are quick and easy to use, such as tagging people or businesses within a post, or liking or sharing content posted by others on LinkedIn. Others may take a bit more effort, such as messaging individual Connections or finding Companies to follow, but that additional effort can be worth it for the insights you gain and the progress you make in strengthening your relationships.

In the next chapter, we'll talk about some more advanced ways to engage with your network and monitor the effectiveness of your LinkedIn participation by taking a strategic approach to content.

18

DEVELOPING A LINKEDIN CONTENT STRATEGY

N ow that you've dipped your toe into the water in terms of participation on LinkedIn by liking, commenting on and sharing posts from your Feed, creating your own Posts, tagging your Connections where appropriate, joining and participating in Groups, it's time to get more strategic about how you use LinkedIn.

There's nothing worse than "random acts of marketing" to create frustration, and the same is true for LinkedIn. This is the reason so many people say that they don't see the value of participating on LinkedIn, or that they don't see results. While engaging in any of the above activities will likely make you a more effective LinkedIn user than your average attorney, to get the most out of your participation on LinkedIn and start seeing real results, you need to engage thoughtfully and consistently. That means developing a content strategy around the goals we talked about way back in Chapter 4.

Digital marketing company Hubspot defines content strategy as, "the management of pretty much any tangible media that you create and own: written, visual, downloadable ... you name it. It is the piece of your marketing plan that continuously demonstrates who you are and the expertise you bring to your industry." We'll extend that for our purposes here not just to content that you create and own, but content that you curate, share and engage with on LinkedIn.

To create your content strategy, you'll want to revisit your purpose for using LinkedIn, and the audience or audiences you are trying to reach and engage with. Your purpose and your audience will dictate your content strategy, which will include deciding the topics or subject matter of content you create or share, the frequency with which you create or share that content, the format of the content (image, text, video, slideshow, document, etc.), and the timing (time of day, day of week, etc.).

For more on this topic, see Allison's Simple Steps column in the March/April 2019 issue of *Law Practice* magazine on developing a basic marketing plan listed in the Resources section at the end of this book.

Using an Editorial Calendar

A helpful tool for developing your content strategy is an editorial calendar. An editorial calendar can help you plan out and keep track of your LinkedIn participation. This can be particularly helpful if you are planning to create long-form content on LinkedIn by using Publisher, which we discuss in more detail below.

Create a posting schedule that includes short updates along with longer pieces of content. Target different audiences with different posts. When should you post? Some experts say the best posting times for LinkedIn are Tuesdays, Wednesdays and Thursdays at 5-6 pm Eastern, but that may vary depending on your audience and time zone. If you monitor your views and likes for posts, you will notice some patterns. For example, if you post late in the evening in the United States and have a global audience of any size, you are likely to see the post start to get traction in Europe and Asia overnight and have built some momentum by morning in the US.

Include LinkedIn Groups as part of your content strategy as well and incorporate Group discussions into your editorial calendar. As discussed in Chapter 15, Groups can be an excellent place to increase your visibility and to establish relationships with targeted groups of people. When you plan your content, create a post or write an article, take the Groups that contain the target audience for that piece of content into account, and share it not only in the Feed, but also with that Group. Or develop a content strategy that includes posts that are created just for individual Groups and not for the Feed.

Vary the posting medium. In addition to text-based posts, you can post links to articles or other content on your website, blog, or other external sites, whether created by you or not; slide presentations from your latest CLE; videos explaining what you do or talking about a case study; photos from a firm event; checklists, one-sheets or other documents, and more.

Writing Articles on LinkedIn using Publisher

As discussed in Chapter 15, LinkedIn allows you to share information with your Network through Posts that appear in the Feed, and in Group discussions. Some of those posts will be original content created by you, and others will be content created by others that is curated or shared by you on LinkedIn (with or without your own commentary attached).

But there is a third way to participate by sharing content on LinkedIn—through writing longer-form posts or articles using LinkedIn's publishing platform. If you want to become a thought leader in a particular area, writing articles is a good way to do that.

In the past, one of the obstacles to be overcome in thought leadership was that it wasn't always so easy to get published, particularly for new legal professionals who might not have as much experience or as many connections, or for solos, who didn't have the budget or other resources to develop their own website or blog.

The LinkedIn publishing platform has largely eliminated all of these concerns. It is (for now) free and easy to write articles and publish them online with LinkedIn's publishing platform. Simply click on the "write an article" link in the share box on your LinkedIn Home page and you will be taken to another area of LinkedIn, called Publisher, which looks just like a word processing program. You may choose to type your article directly into LinkedIn or to write it on an external word processing program and copy and paste it into LinkedIn after it has been completed. Either way, the problem of having a platform or a publisher has been eliminated.

Anatomy of a LinkedIn Article

Header Image

LinkedIn allows you to upload a header image to be featured with your article. This image will be seen both at the top of your article on LinkedIn and with the title of the article in your Activity on your Profile and when the article appears in the Feed. We highly recommend that you add an image to your article, because it makes the article more visible on your Profile and in the Feed. The Publisher header image size is 698 x 400 pixels.

Additional Images

You are also free to add other images throughout your article by clicking on the image icon and uploading images directly into your article. Images can help break up the text, especially for longer articles.

Header

The header of your article on LinkedIn is the title. Click on the designated area and type in the title for your article. This will be seen both in the Feed and under Activity on your Profile. There is a 100-character limit for your title.

Body of the article

The body of the article is the actual content of the article itself. You may choose to post an entirely new article on LinkedIn, or post something that first appeared elsewhere (giving proper attribution, where necessary), such as on your blog or another trade publication. If the article has already appeared elsewhere, especially if it is on a property you "own" (such as your own website or blog), you may wish to post only part of the article or highlights from the article, and then include a link back to the original to drive traffic to your website or blog.

You can include as many relevant links as you like within the article. For example, you may wish to place a brief bio at the bottom of your article and link your name back to your complete bio on your firm website, or link it back to your LinkedIn Profile. Similarly, you may wish to include a call to action in your article with links back to your site, or to other information or resources. For example, if your article covers a topic that is also the subject of a white paper available on your website, your call to action might read something like this, "For more information about how the Medicaid look-back period might affect you, get a copy of our free whitepaper here"—where "here" links to the whitepaper download page.

When you are ready to publish your article, click the blue Publish button. If you are still working, make sure you save your article as a Draft so that you can go back and make changes in the future until you are ready to share it with the LinkedIn community.

You are limited to 40,000 characters for the body of your article. On average, that will be around 8,000 words. That is a very long article.

Sharing Your LinkedIn Article

Posting your article on LinkedIn has the potential to reach a wider audience than your website or blog might have on its own, given the number of people who engage on LinkedIn on a daily basis. In addition, unlike Posts, LinkedIn Articles are indexed by Google. Although Articles do not automatically appear in the Feeds of your Connections as Posts do, your Connections may receive a Notification when you post an article. But you can help promote your article to gain even more visibility in several different ways.

Each article on LinkedIn has its own unique URL, which makes it easy to share on LinkedIn and elsewhere. You can add the article under Publications on your Profile and include its unique link, share the article in a regular post on LinkedIn or in relevant Groups, or on other social media outside of LinkedIn.

One of the best features of the LinkedIn Publisher platform is the great set of analytics you get for each article.

Using LinkedIn Analytics and Other Means to Determine the Effectiveness of Your Strategy

LinkedIn has been adding some tools within the platform to help you see how much attention and engagement you are receiving. This, in turn, can help you to determine how effective your strategy is—are you reaching the right audience? Are your posts getting seen? Are your connections engaging with the content you create or share? Is your audience engaging with your articles?

Who's Viewed Your Profile

The "Who's Viewed Your Profile" feature of LinkedIn now gives you lots of information about the industries and locations of the people who have viewed your Profile, as well as information about how they found you (LinkedIn search, Google search, etc.)—even with a free account (although premium accounts provide even more information).

A quick way to access this information is by clicking on the number next to Who's Viewed Your Profile on the left sidebar of your LinkedIn Home Page.

With a free account, you can see how many times your Profile was viewed over the past ninety days to determine trends. For example, does your Profile garner more views when you post more, or when you post specific kinds of content? Here again, if you use an editorial calendar, it will be easier to gauge the effectiveness of your strategy by simply looking at your editorial calendar to see what kinds of content you posted during that period of time. If you work without a specific strategy or don't plan your content, you'll have to review your activity in LinkedIn to see what you posted during that time.

In "Who's Viewed Your Profile," you can also see a few of the individuals who have looked at your Profile. The amount of information you receive about individuals depends in part on what type of LinkedIn account you have and in part on the settings of the individuals who viewed your Profile. LinkedIn will never invade the settings of its users, so if they are set to "Anonymous" you will not see all of their information even with a premium account.

LinkedIn will usually show you three people who have viewed your Profile with a free account. But you can still get some other useful information from the analytics LinkedIn provides. For example, LinkedIn may tell you that some of the people who looked at your Profile work at a specific company. Or you might find out that several people who looked at your Profile have a specific job title or work in a certain industry.

We discussed the benefits of LinkedIn premium accounts in more detail in Chapter 1, but the information you get on who has viewed your Profile will definitely be one of the features that will make it difficult for you ever to go back to a free account once you've tried a premium account. You get to see (almost) everyone who has viewed your Profile. When job hunting, hiring, checking responses to articles, and the like, this information can be quite useful.

With a premium account, if you send an invitation to someone, you can see that they looked at your Profile. Although they might not accept your invitation, don't take that personally. Some people might check your Profile and then accept your invitation much later. In other cases, you can wait a bit and withdraw the invitation. Often, if someone looks at your Profile and you send them an invitation, they will accept your invitation immediately. While this might feel a bit creepy to you (especially when you know that others probably know that you've viewed their Profile), it can be strategic and might let you know that a referrer, a recruiter, or an event planner has viewed your Profile.

What can you do with this information? For example, if LinkedIn tells you that several people from the same company were looking at your Profile, it might indicate some interest on the part of that company in using your services. Now might be a good time to reach out to any connections you have in that company to see how you might be able to help. At the very least, if that company represents your target audience on LinkedIn, it might indicate that your participation and content strategy is working.

Post and Article Views

The left sidebar of your LinkedIn Home Page will also display information about how many views your recent Posts and Articles have received. Get even more information by clicking on the number displayed, which will take you to your Activity page. Here you can see your Articles, Posts, Documents and other LinkedIn activity. Under each item, you can see the number of views. Click on that number and you will get some additional analytics, such as the titles and locations of those who viewed each item.

You can also navigate to your Articles themselves on LinkedIn to see the statistics for that article. Go to the Articles tab under Activity to get some more detailed analytics about who viewed and reshared your Article, including job title and location.

Be sure to check the features of the premium accounts (which we expect to change and evolve over time) to see if there might be additional analytics that would be important for you. We discussed premium accounts in more detail in Chapter 1.

Company Page Analytics

If you manage a Company Page for your firm, you'll get Analytics on Visitors to your page, the Posts you post to your Page and Followers of your Page.

Under Visitors, you'll see the number of page views, unique visitors, some visitor demographics, and custom button clicks. Under Posts, you'll see the number of views, reactions (like, etc.), comments and shares, as well as impressions (appearances in the Feed), clicks, and engagement rate. Under Followers, you'll get some metrics on the number of new Followers and demographics.

What to do with Analytics Information

Take note of who is engaging with your content on LinkedIn and engage back with them; view their Profile and their Activity on LinkedIn and share or comment on it. Send a LinkedIn Message to start a private conversation.

Use analytics to find out what content LinkedIn likes the best or what performs the best. What content gets you the most engagement? Experiment with both the substantive content and the format of the post. Do posts with images do better? Does adding hashtags to your post improve engagement? Do videos get more views than other types of content? Are people you tag in your posts engaging with your content? Can you identify and track some key performance metrics that will give you valuable and actionable information?

Planning, developing and executing a content strategy takes some time and effort, but it may be the most important thing you do to improve your LinkedIn results, whether you are hiring LinkedIn to expand your network, increase your visibility, or to encourage referrals. By taking a deliberate approach to what, when, where and how you post and reviewing your analytics to see what kinds of content resonates with your target audience, you are sure to become a go-to member of your network.

19

ADVANCED AND POWER USER TIPS: PARTICIPATION

We've covered a lot of ground so far in our third essential building block, but here are a few additional tips to really maximize your LinkedIn participation.

Sometimes it's easier to sit down and create a bunch of posts at once, instead of logging in to LinkedIn every day. As we mentioned in the previous chapter, you can do this by using an editorial calendar to plan out and schedule your LinkedIn content. Another tool you can use to make this even easier is a scheduling tool like Hootsuite (***http://www.hootsuite.com***). A scheduling tool will allow you to schedule LinkedIn Posts in advance and keep your Profile updated, even when you are not logged in. If you participate in other social networks, including Facebook and Twitter, using Hootsuite will allow you to send Posts to multiple networks at once, all in one place.

Create a LinkedIn SlideShare account and upload presentations (or portions of presentations if you don't want to give them all away), then add them to your Profile or send Posts or Articles on LinkedIn that link back to your SlideShare presentations. According to LinkedIn, over 4 million people visit LinkedIn SlideShare daily, and Google indexes all presentations on the platform.

Take your online relationships offline—use LinkedIn to identify people with whom you can have lunch or coffee to get to know them better and find out how you can help them. Invite Connections to attend a seminar or event with you.

Schedule regular weekly or monthly time for LinkedIn activities, including visiting your LinkedIn Home page, accepting connection invitations, sending thank-yous or other messages through LinkedIn, and participating in Group discussions.

Regularly check LinkedIn for information about industries, clients, and potential clients and set up LinkedIn tools to bring you relevant information on a regular basis. Follow companies, individuals and influencers whose content is valuable to you and your network.

Use self-promotion sparingly, self-deprecatingly, and subtly on LinkedIn. Always think about the actual value to others you bring and think about how you would react to someone else doing the same thing. The 80/20 rule will stand you in good stead: your posts should be 80% informational and only 20% promotional—but even promotional posts should add value to your network.

Sync your blog and Twitter accounts to LinkedIn to allow for cross-posting and to get a bigger audience for information you post in other places. If you cannot connect them automatically, use tools like Zapier or IFTTT to connect them.

Use "Congratulate" links in LinkedIn email notifications to acknowledge new jobs and other changes for your Connections. Personalize the message to make it even more memorable.

Because LinkedIn allows you to interact with fellow Group members easily, even if they are outside of your Network, use Groups as a way to meet new people and make Connections.

Even if you're not ready to connect or converse, "Follow" individuals of interest to you within a Group to receive their Posts. This is a great way to see what experts in your field are saying even though you are not connected to them.

Use LinkedIn's analytics tools to see who is engaging with your content and engage back with them.

Tag LinkedIn users with whom you would like to establish or continue a relationship to help them to engage with your Posts.

Watch what LinkedIn power users are doing—what are they posting? When? How often? What do their posts look like? See what ideas you can steal from them.

Vary the types of posts you make: entertain, engage, inform, advise—and the post format—text, image, video, etc.

For even more interest, add stickers and text to your video through the mobile app by selecting the sticker or text icons near the video before you post.

Repurpose articles you've written—both on and off of LinkedIn—into shorter LinkedIn posts and schedule them for future posting. You can choose to link to the complete article or just leave your post as a stand-alone "nugget" of value for your Network.

Use images with your content as often as you can—when scrolling through the Feed, posts with images will stand out more.

Post video—LinkedIn, like many other platforms, is prioritizing video content, so get out there and shoot video. You don't need any fancy equipment or a professional studio; video taken from your laptop or smartphone will do. Keep videos short for more engagement.

Share documents (PDF, slides, papers and reports) not just on your Profile, but within Groups and through the Feed (As of the time this book was published, this is only available on desktop, although LinkedIn promises to roll it out on mobile soon)—and don't forget to add a title (58 characters or less).

20

FREQUENTLY ASKED QUESTIONS: PARTICIPATION

How do I find Groups to join?

There are several different ways to find Groups to join on LinkedIn. The easiest is to do a search of groups that you already belong to in the offline world. For example, your local bar association, your law school alumni, and your local chamber of commerce may have LinkedIn Groups. If you are already a part of those communities, they are easy places to start.

But you can also search for Groups on LinkedIn based on your interests or subject matter—simply type in the search box and then click on "see all results for…". When you're taken to the next (advanced search) page, click on the More button, and then click Groups to search just for Groups. For example, Allison is a member of Groups on LinkedIn for women in business, legal marketing and more.

A third way you can find Groups to join is by looking at the Groups your Connections—especially those Connections who represent your target market on LinkedIn—belong to. You can see what Groups a connection belongs to by navigating to their Profile and scrolling down until you see the Interests box. This portion of the Profile shows the Influencers, Companies, Groups and Schools that are followed by your Connection. To see just the Groups, click on See All at the bottom of the box, and click on the Groups tab.

What should I post in Groups?

The thought process for posting in Groups is similar to the posts that you would add to the Feed, only more targeted. Here, your audience is obviously only the Group members, so everything you post to the Feed may not be a good fit for every Group you belong to. But we think posting to Groups is an often-overlooked way to gain more visibility for you and your posts. Many times, the Group membership is much larger than your own network, so it is a good idea to keep your Groups in mind when you post.

If you're not sure whether a particular post makes sense for a specific Group, navigate to the Group's page and read the Group's rules. Look at what other people are posting in the Group and what kinds of posts get the most engagement.

How often should I post on LinkedIn? Won't I annoy my network if I post too much?

There is no hard and fast rule on this—much of it depends on who your connections are and why you are using LinkedIn. But it also depends on the quality of your posts. Users on LinkedIn are participating for business reasons. Most LinkedIn users don't appreciate a barrage of Posts about your meals or personal activities—those are more the province of Twitter or Facebook. But if you provide value and quality, posting daily or even more frequently isn't too often.

Keep in mind that your connections are not going to see all of your Posts unless they choose to go to your Profile and look at all of your activity. Most Posts won't last long on a user's Home Feed, and the more connections they have, the less likely it is that they will see your Post. LinkedIn doesn't send your Network notifications every time you post. And LinkedIn's algorithms, especially in the mobile app, is determining what posts people see in their Feeds by defaulting to "Top" as opposed to "Recent" posts.

Won't it sound like I'm bragging if I post about what I'm doing on LinkedIn?

It's all in the delivery. Before you post on LinkedIn, you want to make sure that there is something about the post that would be helpful or interesting to your Connections, and write it in such a way that it provides value. Think about why your Network would care about what you are going to post. Is the information relevant to them? Does it say something about how you might be able to help them? For example, perhaps your Connections don't all know about all of the services you provide to your clients. If that's the case, it might be helpful for them to see a post about the fact that you just completed a successful commercial real estate transaction for a client.

A good approach is to link to a news story about your success, mention it in a post where you congratulate someone else involved in the transaction, or post a photo of a group celebrating the success. Photos make a big difference in engagement. Dennis has done some experimenting and believes that adding a photo of others tends to draw the largest numbers of views and likes. For example, if Dennis posts a photo of himself teaching his class and a post with a photo of the students of the class, even with the same message, the post with the photo of the students is likely to get two or three times the number of views. Do some experimenting of your own.

Can I request Endorsements from my Connections?

No—or at least not easily. Although you can send Recommendation requests to your LinkedIn Connections, you cannot request Endorsements from your Connections by simply clicking a button. If you wish to request an Endorsement, you would need to contact your Connection directly, either with a LinkedIn Message, by email, or when you speak with them to ask them to Endorse you by going to your LinkedIn Profile and clicking the + next to the Skill you'd like the Endorsement for.

When is the best time to request a Recommendation on LinkedIn?

We think the best—and easiest—time to request a Recommendation on LinkedIn is when someone pays you a compliment or thanks you for work you have done for them. If you receive a great email from a client expressing their gratitude or singing your praises, ask if they wouldn't mind writing the same for you on LinkedIn. When someone says, "Let me know if there is anything I can do for you," suggesting that they write you a Recommendation may be just the thing. Remember, however, that like reference letters, Recommendations take a lot of time and work on the part of the recommender.

How do you send a message to only a subset of your Connections?

Regular Posts on LinkedIn are seen by all of your connections (unless they elect otherwise), but you can send messages to subsets of your connections. The current process is a manual one. Again, this feature is a useful one and it might show up in Premium accounts, although we do not see that it is available as of the time this book was published. You can send messages to multiple recipients by adding their names separately into the "to" field when you create your message. On the mobile app, you'll go to your Messages, click + to add a new message, and then click the icon to compose a group message and type all of your recipients' names.

When you send a message to multiple recipients, they will be able to see that it was a group message, and all replies within the conversation will be seen by all recipients.

Messages will arrive in your connections' Inbox on LinkedIn, and—depending on their LinkedIn Settings—they will also receive an email.

PART V

CONCLUSION: PLANNING YOUR LINKEDIN ACTIVITY

21

A BASIC LINKEDIN ACTION PLAN FOR EVERYONE

Congratulations! You have learned about the three essential building blocks of LinkedIn that you must master: Profiles, Connections, and Participation. You should also be seeing the important of having a LinkedIn strategy and know the answer to the question, "What job are you hiring LinkedIn to do for you?" We hope that you now see how LinkedIn both tracks and enhances the networking you do in the real world. Now it is time to put together a basic plan for moving your LinkedIn game to the next level and making LinkedIn work for you.

PROFILE

If you're a beginner, or if your Profile hasn't yet reached "All Star" status, spend 30 minutes each week improving your Profile until you reach "All Star" status.

Start by:

► Creating a well-crafted Headline considering the perspective of your target audience (ex: title, firm name, practice areas or services you provide to clients) and asking several people you know if your new Headline accurately describes you in an engaging way

- ► Completing your Summary
- ► Improving the descriptions of your current and two former positions

Next steps—add:

- ► Skills, at least six. Check with some friends, clients or colleagues to confirm that these skills match the skills that they associate with you
- ► Honors and awards—don't forget about community awards or awards that people think of in positive ways, like Eagle Scout
- ► Organizations, Publications, Volunteer work, etc.

Spend 10 minutes each week on maintenance. Or, if you're already a LinkedIn "All Star," don't stop there—spend at least 30 minutes initially to brainstorm other sections or multi-media elements you can add to your Profile. Update as necessary with new info as it arises, including media, publications, and the like. And don't forget to replace an old photo with something newer and better.

CONNECTIONS

Beginners, spend 15 minutes each week working on your Connections.

Start by:

- ► Responding to existing invitations in your inbox. It's OK to ignore invitations from people you don't know
- ► Uploading your Outlook or other address book (make sure to check "deselect all" before sending invitations)

► Send personalized invitations to six to ten people a day for a week and track your results

Next steps—Look for people to connect with using:

► People You May Know

► Alumni

► Search for specific terms, companies, or geographies

If you're not a beginner, you still need to spend time updating and maintaining your connections. Spend 10-15 minutes each week on maintenance.

► Invite new real-world contacts to connect with you on LinkedIn

► Send personalized notes and private messages (continue the conversation) to people who accept your invitation

► Determine whether you want to create a goal of a certain number of Connections in a certain period of time

PARTICIPATION

Participation is the real value of participating on LinkedIn. Beginners and experienced LinkedIn users should spend 30 minutes each week participating on LinkedIn.

Start by:

► Finding at least 3 Groups to join (choose groups, like alumni, you already belong to, or choose groups your clients belong to in real life)

- ► Posting to your Feed once or twice a week with content that would be interesting to your audience
- ► Liking, commenting or sharing others' Posts from your Home page

Next steps:

- ► Start discussions/post articles of interest to your Groups
- ► Write articles on LinkedIn (or repurpose articles you've written elsewhere) using LinkedIn Publisher

On an ongoing basis, you can:

- ► Send at least one Post/week
- ► Review Group discussions and join in
- ► Review your Home page for content ideas to share
- ► React to others' Posts

Don't forget to take your LinkedIn relationships offline. Remember that LinkedIn shouldn't exist in a vacuum; it is an extension of your "real-world" networking. Just as you should transfer your in-person and existing relationships to LinkedIn, you should transfer the relationships you establish on LinkedIn into the real world. Schedule a phone call or a meeting with your Connections to take your relationship to the next level.

PART VI

MAKING LINKEDIN
WORK FOR YOU

22

BUILDING YOUR PERSONAL BRAND ON LINKEDIN

Your law firm or organization's brand is a reflection not just of the work the firm does, but also its culture, its values, and how the firm interacts with and services its clients. The firm's brand is its personality.

Similarly, a personal brand is an expression of who you are as an individual, what you stand for, and what value you bring to your clients, referral sources, and your network. Your personal brand is unique because you are a unique individual. No one else has exactly the same skills, the same experiences, connections and values, or the same personal story. Your personal brand is what distinguishes you from your competitors and even from other legal professionals in your firm or organization who do what you do.

You may have heard it said that people do business with individuals, not necessarily with firms or organizations. That may be especially true for legal professionals, because of the nature of the problems legal professionals solve for their clients. Even business clients want to work with legal professionals who they know, like and trust.

LinkedIn provides legal professionals with a unique opportunity to build a personal brand online, whether they are an associate in a large firm, a solo practitioner, a paralegal, in house counsel, or a brand-new lawyer or law student still seeking a job, and even if they do not have their own website or other "real estate" on the internet. While law firms and other organizations have an opportunity to create Company Pages and Showcase Pages LinkedIn, it does not appear as of the date of publication of this book that too many people follow Company Pages. But they do follow individuals.

Even if you are a solo, a strong personal brand is an asset to your firm. For example, think about people like Guy Kawasaki, Oprah Winfrey, and Marie Forleo. They each have strong personal brands and many people follow them as influencers even if they don't follow or interact with the companies they represent. The individual's brand and story is so strong that it creates interest even separate from their business.

To build your personal brand on LinkedIn, you'll want to bring together all of the elements we've already discussed in this book into one authentic, cohesive story about who you are professionally, what you have already accomplished and what you hope to accomplish in the future. This is a story that may change and evolve over time, depending on what you are hiring LinkedIn to do for you, but keeping your personal brand in mind when you do your regular review of your LinkedIn Profile, Connections and Participation can help you decide what you may wish to add, update, change or eliminate.

Is Your Personal Brand Clearly Represented in Your Profile?

Let's start with the first essential building block: your LinkedIn Profile. Take another look at your Profile to see how you can make it stand out. We've already talked in Chapters 6 and 7 about how to develop your Profile using keywords and write to capture the interest of your target audience. Looking at your Profile as a whole, does it capture your unique story and highlight your value? Does it convey what brought you to the law or to your area of practice and what you are known for?

Does your headline grab the attention of your target audience? Does your About section accurately sum up what you do and who you do it for? Does your Experience section provide your target audience with a comprehensive look at your background, rather than a dry list of tasks you've performed at previous jobs? Do your featured Skills line up with your Headline, Experience and About sections?

Consider other elements of your Profile as well. Have you added a background photo to your Profile? Does that photo create a compelling story about who you are? Does your LinkedIn headshot align with the story you're telling on your Profile? Does it depict you as you would like clients to see you? Have you included other images on your profile that support your personal brand? Have you posted videos or slide presentations that establish your expertise or convey authority? Can you include documents, checklists, flowcharts or other materials that help to demonstrate your brand story?

Does your LinkedIn presence convey strong third-party support for your personal brand? What do others typically come to you for advice about or recognize as your area of expertise? Are these reflected in your Profile? Are you receiving Endorsements for the Skills that are most closely associated with your personal brand story? Do you have Recommendations on your Profile from trusted clients, colleagues and others that demonstrate the qualities of your personal brand?

Connections Reflect Your Personal Brand

Believe it or not, your LinkedIn Connections are also part of your personal brand on LinkedIn. When you look at your Connections on LinkedIn, do they tell the story of who you are as a professional? Are you connected with or following influencers that align with your brand?

Does the number of your LinkedIn Connections reflect how robust your network is or does it make you look like a bit of a hermit? Are there gaps that need to be filled in? For example, are you connected to former employers, colleagues and classmates? Are your professional Connections outside of the law represented as well, for example, vendors, community contacts, and contacts from charity or volunteer work?

Do your LinkedIn Connections help to expose you to more of the kinds of people you would like to meet or connect with both on LinkedIn and in the outside world? Do you actively build your brand awareness by looking at who your Connections are connected to and asking for introductions? Do you help your Connections by making introductions to others in your Network who might be able to help them in their careers? Use LinkedIn to help you find potential connections with whom you can collaborate to extend your personal brand.

Supporting Your Personal Brand with your LinkedIn Participation

Finally, what can you share with your LinkedIn audience in posts, comments and articles to help them remember you? What value do you bring to the table and how is it demonstrated through your activity on LinkedIn? What are you the 'go-to' person for, and is that reflected in your posts and other activity?

Build your authority, your brand, and your engagement with LinkedIn users both inside and outside of your Network by using the many publishing opportunities presented on LinkedIn, whether through individual Posts and Company Updates, posting in Groups and joining discussions, writing longer-form content on LinkedIn Publisher, or creating a LinkedIn SlideShare account for your presentations. Since SlideShare gets millions of visitors per day, it can be a powerful brand-building and brand awareness tool.

Personal Brand and Job Search

Looking for a job? Building a strong personal brand on LinkedIn can help set you apart from other candidates. Ensure that your LinkedIn Summary or About statement is well-written and summarizes your skills, how you have used them in the past, whether in school, for a previous employer, or as part of an internship or clinical program, how those skills can help a future employer, and what makes you different from other potential candidates. Gather as many examples as possible that demonstrate the high-quality work you can do, whether those are presentations for a law school class, articles written for your law school or bar association paper, or a (redacted) motion written as part of an internship, and post them on LinkedIn. Write articles in Publisher on news stories that impact your area of interest in the legal field. Connect with prominent local legal professionals in the area of practice you aspire to work in.

A potential employer cannot help but sit up and take notice of a candidate who has developed a LinkedIn presence that clearly represents who they are and what they can offer to an employer, and who has actively demonstrated that he or she is already beginning to build connections and is enthusiastically following their area of interest.

It's Your Brand

Like it or not, you have a personal brand that dictates how other people perceive, respond, and react to you both online and in the real world. You should take charge of your personal brand by being proactive and strategic about what you post and how you engage with others on LinkedIn so that their perception matches what you want it to be, and so that you stand out from others who do what you do.

Take some time to review your LinkedIn Profile, Connections and Participation to see how they enhance or detract from your personal brand, and then make a plan going forward to ensure that everything you do on LinkedIn advances your personal brand. Ask yourself questions like those above an incorporate your answers into your LinkedIn presence. As Tom Peters has said, "the brand is You!" Is your LinkedIn presence telling your brand story?

23

LINKEDIN FOR JOB SEARCH

inkedIn is the premier tool today for job search. Most
employers post open positions on LinkedIn, and many
recruiters say that LinkedIn has already replaced the
traditional resume. In fact, your Profile works as a living resume
that is available on the Internet 24 hours a day, seven days a week,
whether or not you are looking for a job.

LinkedIn even allows you to convert your Profile into a professional-looking standard PDF resume automatically, and your resume should include the URL for your LinkedIn Profile..

LinkedIn has a full set of tools for job seekers, mostly available
through one of its premium plans. The Premium Career plan offers
several features designed for job seekers: expanded ability to see
who has viewed your Profile, Job Insights, and Salary Insights. But
there are several features in the free version of LinkedIn that you
can use to research companies or firms that are seeking to hire,
find out how you might be connected to that firm or company and
who you might know who is also employed there, see what Groups
they're following or what they find of interest on LinkedIn. You can
follow the company or firm's Company Page to get their Updates.
It's difficult to imagine looking for a job today and not using LinkedIn.

Three Steps to Start

If you are looking for a job, you will want to do three things to start, no matter what your plan or strategy is:

1. Use your LinkedIn Jobs page. Simply click on the "Jobs" tab on the top navigation bar in the desktop version, or on the Jobs icon that looks like a briefcase in the mobile app and you will be taken to a dashboard with all sorts of job search tools. It will be the best way to look for position openings that have been posted. Use it as the home page for your job search.

2. Purchase the Premium Career plan for the duration of your job search. The cost is $25 per month and you get additional tools and settings to make yourself visible to recruiters.

3. Update your Profile, especially your Headline.

Strategic Focus

Next, you will want to focus on your strategy. What are you hiring LinkedIn to do for your job search? It's easy to think that the answer is "to find me a new job." That's vague and nebulous. It's actually difficult to translate that job into practical action steps. However, the more precise and nuanced your answer to that question is, the more LinkedIn can help you. If you want to find open positions in local law firms that have been posted and for which applications are being accepted, you'll take one approach. If you are targeting certain potential employers, you will take another approach.

Consider this: in many cases, the job you want to hire LinkedIn to do is actually to help you get interviews for potential jobs. In that case, adding Connections, talking to influencers, finding shared Connections, targeting Posts, and other tactics will become important.

Plan in Advance

You will want to start your efforts on LinkedIn in advance of your actual job search, if you can. Ask questions like:

- ► What would an excellent candidate for the role that you are seeking look like? Does your LinkedIn presence make you look like that candidate?
- ► Are you connected to thought leaders in your community?
- ► Are you connected to legal professionals and others in the organizations you are targeting?
- ► Does your Profile contain the right keywords and terms used by people in the field?
- ► Are you sending useful content and sharing links to great information in your Posts?

In many cases, the information you provide and the Connections you have within the client base (especially for business lawyers) will be more important that what you are showing in the legal space. Develop a plan and work it.

Alumni and Former Colleagues

Growing and nurturing your network of alumni contacts and former colleagues can be an important step in your job search. Note that if you went to a small college, alumni Connections can be especially strong and helpful ones. In cities like St. Louis, where you went to high school is incredibly important. You might add your high school and even high school achievements to your Profile for your job search.

Groups and Networking

Joining LinkedIn Groups can be another effective strategy. Look for groups that contain keywords used in the jobs that you are looking for. For example, if you want a data privacy law position in Chicago, a group called something like "Chicago Data Privacy Lawyers," if it is active, could be a tremendous resource.

In other words, you want to look carefully at all three of the essential building blocks of LinkedIn and improve your effectiveness in each of them.

Networking is unquestionably the best way to get jobs these days, even though it's easy to fall into the habit of simply applying for posted jobs. Use LinkedIn to request introductions, connect to people you already know (or who know you) at a prospective employer, learn more about people you interview with, and to find people who are willing to help you and give you advice. It takes time and work but will have the additional benefit of reconnecting with people you've known in the past who are still willing to help you.

Company Pages

LinkedIn Company Pages are a great way to research an organization, its clients and customers, its people, and its culture. It would be a huge mistake not to review the Profiles of the people who will be interviewing you in advance. That should be seen as a standard part of interview preparation. Think about the benefit of starting an interview with "Our mutual friend, X, says to tell you hello."

Learning Resources

LinkedIn has a lot of learning tools and other resources that can help you prepare for interviews and get up-to-speed in subjects you might feel a little rusty on. Simply click on the icon for "Learning" in the top navigation bar and you'll see the wide range of offerings that are available. Some require a premium account, which is one reason we recommend considering purchasing the Premium Career account when you are actively looking for a new job.

There are many resources out there about using LinkedIn for job hunting, so we won't go into much detail. We'll end this chapter, with answers to questions we often get about using LinkedIn while job hunting.

Frequently Asked Questions: Job Hunting and LinkedIn

What should I do if I don't currently have a job?

In a sense, every unemployed lawyer has a solo practice, even if they don't actually have any clients yet. Rather than leaving a gap or showing that you are unemployed, consider listing your current "job" as your own law practice or consulting business. In some cases, it might make sense to say that you are "changing careers" or even "taking a career break" or "actively considering new options."

Be positive about what you say and make it sound like you have made a choice about what you are doing.

Should I include in my Headline that I am looking for a job?

If you are currently employed and connected to your colleagues, you probably will want to avoid this. In some other settings, "BigLaw corporate senior associate seeking in-house counsel position" or "family lawyer relocating to Georgia looking for progressive family law firm" might make sense. We like the approach some law students use, saying "looking for challenging 2L summer associate position in IP firm." There are many right answers here. And you can always test some different approaches from time to time. Our best advice is to change your Headline to describe what you do best and want you want to do. For example, "innovative estate planning attorney focusing on digital assets and cryptocurrency issues" will be much better than "senior associate at X law firm."

As an aside, in most organizations, people tend to assume that every time you have a "dentist appointment," you are interviewing, and that "getting a crown" means that you are having second and follow-up interviews. People will assume what they assume. If you suddenly become active on LinkedIn, most people assume that you are looking for a job. It's better to establish that you have a regular cadence of updating if you want to hide that you are currently looking than to suddenly start sending daily Posts.

Should I remove dates, not list old jobs, or hide old jobs, awards and the like from viewers, especially if they reveal my age?

We get these questions all the time. First, when you remove dates, people, rightly or wrongly, assume you do it because you are concerned that you are too old (or too young). You might actually accentuate the issue. Gaps in resumes can trigger concerns about what happened during that time period. More important, eliminating this information effectively blocks people from finding your shared commonalities, experiences, former colleagues, and alumni. There is also a good chance that, during the application process, you will have to disclose these things anyway. Ultimately, it is a personal decision. As an example, Dennis resists the common advice not to include anything from high school, in large part because, early in his career, he did not put "Eagle Scout" on his resume and had several mentors tell him that they would have hired him on the spot if Eagle Scout would have been on his resume. Think it through carefully but realize that today's standard advice is to remove dates that reveal your age. Interestingly, this advice is given both to young and to old people.

Do I have to list every single job I had?

Again, you want to make a tactical choice. If you had a job in high school where you worked at a zoo, you might keep that in your Profile forever. It's a great interview conversation-starter. One option is to "bundle" experiences, which can be a good thing for students. You might not want to list every fast food restaurant you worked at, but you can be effective by listing them as a "bundle"—"various jobs with increasing responsibility in the food services and restaurant industry"—and list some key skills, especially if you've managed people, had to meet deadlines, or the like. You'd be surprised what the person looking at your Profile and you might have in common or how a hiring partner might value someone who met deadlines and worked under pressure in any job.

Should I send Posts with photos of me working, getting awards, or participating in community events?

Yes, keeping in mind your confidentiality obligations to clients. People respond well to photos and you will see more likes, comments, and shares when your Post contains a photo. Imagine starting an interview with the interviewer saying, "I liked that picture of you receiving that award for that Girls Who Code project."

Is there a way to mention past jobs without adding them as a job in my experience section?

The pro tip here is to mention them in your About section only, and not enter them as separate Positions under Experience.

Can I create two (or more) LinkedIn accounts during a job search and tailor each of them to what I want?

Having more than one account violates LinkedIn's terms of service. In addition, it can cause a lot of confusion for people. The better approach is to be strategic in how you write your Headline and Summary (About), in what order you list your current positions, and what you highlight with audio, video, and links.

What about mentioning potentially controversial topics or identifying race, gender, LGBTQ+ status, political or religious affiliation, or anything else that might turn off a potential employer?

That is a big question and one that we are often asked. Ultimately, you need to decide what you are comfortable with. The fact is that hiding these things from a potential employer who is discriminatory or who will have a negative approach might mean that you get the job, but the odds are that you will not stay at that job for very long and it is likely to be a bad experience. On the other hand, some people clearly have good reasons not to reveal certain things. It's a tradeoff: does revealing something open up more and better opportunities than it closes? There is definitely no one-size-fits-all answer. In large part, you will want to consider what you do in the real world.

If I am changing careers from a different profession to law, should I start a new account and concentrate just on legal Connections?

No. Your existing Connections could still lead you to potential clients. Also, your current Connections will be excited about your career change and willing to help you. Think in terms of adding a new legal addition to your current house of Connections.

Is LinkedIn a good place to make a first contact in job searching? Or should I use LinkedIn as a follow up only after applying for a job in a traditional setting?

Both. However, remember that LinkedIn is also a great way to prepare the ground for talking to a potential employer by building out Connections in advance at that employer.

As for connecting with an individual on LinkedIn as your first contact, that's a complex topic, and one on which we have somewhat different views. Allison wouldn't recommend it if you're seeking a position with that firm, although if you are simply seeking information and not actively seeking employment from a particular individual, connecting on LinkedIn might be OK. Dennis thinks that, while it has long been the accepted etiquette not to connect with someone interviewing you until after the job decision has been made, it is more common to receive connection invitations from job applicants during the hiring and interview process in the last year or so.

There is going to be some risk of awkwardness or even a negative reaction (and it's difficult to know how to interpret the fact that someone does not accept your invitation), so you want to give some thought to the approach. It's an interesting strategy and one you might consider if you see that someone who is involved in the hiring process has looked at your Profile.

Another direct approach is simply to ask at the end of the interview if you can send a LinkedIn invitation. A final thought: sending a LinkedIn message or a personalized invitation is a good alternative to the traditional thank you email.

As a new attorney searching for a job would you recommend that I request to connect with employers?

See our answer to the previous question. As a new attorney or student, it might be more important to find likely Connections (especially alumni) at the employer. It does make sense to follow the employer's Company Page, if they have one. Try to find the in-between connections that make sense. Look at the employer contact's list of contacts and see if there are people you know. Connect to them. Then when the employer looks at your Profile, they'll notice that you have shared connections and that might give you something to talk about in an interview. Or the shared connection might be able to put in a good word for you.

Can your current employer see you are a job seeker?

They may see that you have a premium account but there is no logo or alert that would indicate that you have a Premium Career account. If you don't want your network to know that you're looking for a job, you may want to check your settings. An important one to remember is to turn off the notifications that you have updated your Profile. It's a dead giveaway when notices of every update you make to your Profile go out to all your Connections. If you're in a job seeker group, you may want to choose settings so that group does not appear on your Profile. No updates will go to your network if you apply for a job through LinkedIn. Do you really think your current boss will be looking at your Profile?

Could you put what you're seeking in the About section, maybe by mentioning what your skills are in a paragraph and then the position you are seeking?

We give you permission to be as creative as you want to be in your About section. The About section is a good place to describe your interests and what you're seeking in a position, as well as what would qualify you as a good candidate for that position, just as your cover letter would when sending out a resume. We like to think of the About section as an online form of cover letter or, as it used to be called, a summary of all of your experience to date.

Can I use my listing of Skills to help in my job search?

You can and you should. You will want to revisit your Skill selections, put them in the order that will appeal most to potential employers, and hide or change the order they present. By the way, as we mention elsewhere in this book, Skills are a great feedback system in LinkedIn. You can see what people think you do and make adjustments. In a job search, I would ask close Connections to up-vote certain Skills for you.

Happy job hunting!

24

LINKEDIN FOR LAW STUDENTS

We love talking with law students about LinkedIn. LinkedIn lets law students create and build a strong professional presence while in law school. We have also seen law students land great jobs largely due to their use of LinkedIn.

Unfortunately, many law students are still getting advice from law professors, career services people, legal professionals, and others that should either stay off LinkedIn or use it in very limited ways. The advice is usually framed in the context that "what goes on the Internet stays there permanently" and implies that law students will inevitably do something embarrassing. We will avoid making the snarky comment that much of that advice seems to come from people who barely use LinkedIn. In any event, the advice also misunderstands LinkedIn's role as a professional networking platform.

We do have two over-arching rules for law students using LinkedIn: be professional and show good judgment. Not surprisingly, those are the same rules that we have for everyone else.

If you are a law student who has read the rest of this book, you will undoubtedly already have many ideas for using LinkedIn while you are in law school.

Here are some of our best tips and FAQs specifically for law students:

Tips

1. **Start adding Connections early**. During law school, it's a great time to get your Connection list up to date. Your college professors, advisors, deans, former employers, high school teachers, organization leaders, parents' friends and business associates, your friends' parents, and many others will be happy (and perhaps even flattered) to connect on LinkedIn. There is currently a trend of Millennials moving to LinkedIn and away from Facebook. Add current and former classmates as Connections because they are people who will refer business to you if they know what you do.

2. **Work Your Alumni Connections**. In many cases, especially with small colleges, all alumni like to be helpful to recent graduates. Asking a fellow alumnus to connect on LinkedIn is one of the easiest asks you can make and one of the easiest for an alumnus to grant. You will want to start to stockpile these Connections to activate later. Similarly, law school alumni Connections will also be helpful. Spend a little time looking for alumni at potential employers and in your fields of interest. Personalized invitations are an absolute must here, as are thank yous.

3. **Invitations to Guest Speakers**. Something that we encourage law students to do (and regret that we hadn't done more of) is to take advantage of the great slate of legal guest speakers on campus during your time in school. If you attend a session, introduce yourself to the speaker afterwards and ask a question or two. Also ask them if they would be willing to connect on LinkedIn.

This simple effort can build the quality of your LinkedIn network and potentially open doors.

4. **Keep Working on Your Profile**. Make your professional Headline as distinctive as possible, depending on what you want to get out of LinkedIn. Your Headline can include that you are a student (and perhaps even your year), the school you attend, the positions you're seeking or area of law you're interested in. If you have relevant school assignments, articles, or work done during a summer job or internship, include them on your Profile as well. Here's another idea: look at a lot of law student profiles from your school and elsewhere. Which ones do you like the best? Which ones would you like the best if you were a hiring partner or a recruiter? Make your Headline look like the ones that you like best.

5. **Take LinkedIn into the Real World**. We've seen LinkedIn create many opportunities for law students: invitations to conferences, fellowships to associations, blog writing and co-authoring articles, lunch and coffee invitations, and much more. LinkedIn is just the start. The power and the benefits for your career come when you follow up in the real world.

Frequently Asked Questions

1. **How much should I say about a prior career outside of law?** List your previous career and then use the About section of your Profile as a way to highlight the ways in which the knowledge, skills and experience that you gained in your previous career will stand you in good stead in your legal career, how they might help

you to understand your clients better or help them in ways that others who don't have that experience might not be able to do. Or use the About section to talk about why you made the change and how your previous experience informed your decision to go into law. Many law firms really do value prior business or work experience, especially in some of the more specialized areas of law. Evidence of leadership, management experience, awards, successful projects and other experience can be helpful in getting interviews and distinguishing yourself from other candidates.

2. **What should I do if I have no legal experience to put on my Profile?** You will want to focus on skills and experience that transfer to law. Public speaking, writing, leadership, management, and many other skills are part of being a lawyer. You might also highlight undergraduate classes on legal topics, list the law school classes that you have taken and are taking, any internships, externships, summer jobs or part time positions you've held while you're in school, and showcase any special projects, clinical programs or writing you've done while you're in law school.

3. **What's the worst advice you've heard for law students?** There are a number of choices, but the one we want to highlight is that 1Ls and 2Ls should not post anything on LinkedIn because they don't know enough law and will only embarrass themselves. In fact, we know students who have posted class papers on LinkedIn which have led directly to job offers.

This advice also misses one of the key points about LinkedIn that we cover in the Participation section: you do not need to publish original content or even legal content to provide valuable information to your network. Dennis met a 1L who already knows that he wants to do something in the area of supply chain law. This student never needs to publish anything original on supply chain law, but if they send regular Posts about supply chain legal and business topics and build out connections in that field, by the time they graduate they will likely be known as a "supply chain legal expert." We would argue that that would be much more valuable than posting one link to a law review article on an esoteric legal topic.

4. **On the subject of posting original content, do you have any recommendations?** We live in a world where short is better accepted than long. If you've written a paper for a class that got at least a B, get some editing help and post it as a LinkedIn article. If the paper is one that demonstrates a high level of knowledge or expertise in a specific area, and that area is one in which you are seeking employment, it might be worthwhile to publish the entire paper. Just because you post it doesn't mean that anyone is going to read the entire paper, but there might be advantages to seeing that you've published something that substantial. If you're posting it as an example of your writing ability or style, you might want to ask yourself whether you'd provide the entire paper or just a portion as a writing sample to accompany a job application or resume. You can divide the paper into segments and post each segment as a separate article to get even more mileage out of it. Or you could write a short version of the article. Or you can create a "listicle" (5 things you need to know about X) from your paper, or create several shorter posts with the main points in your paper. Look for ways to repurpose your best work.

Be smart about LinkedIn as a student. Don't be put off by well-intentioned naysayers. Instead, look to law students who have had success using LinkedIn. They will be willing to share their stories and their advice.

25

MOVING TO A NEW PRACTICE AREA OR LOCATION

We live in a culture in which relocations and career changes are commonplace. LinkedIn can be a big help in making both kinds of moves.

Dennis recently moved from St. Louis (after 35 years) to Ann Arbor, Michigan. Using LinkedIn was an important part of the pre-move and post-move process.

There are legal professionals who have made plans to move to a new practice area or new geographic area and set up the moves several years in advance, with LinkedIn playing a major role.

Both scenarios illustrate our approach to LinkedIn: having a clear strategy focusing on the job to be done and smartly using each of the three essential LinkedIn building blocks. In many ways, these approaches are similar to what we suggested for law students.

Your broad strategy is pretty easy to state: you want to move to a new location or practice area.

The key part of your strategy will be focusing with precision on the job to be done. For example, you might want to use LinkedIn to activate your existing network in the new location and leverage them to expand your network before you move. You might want to become something of a thought leader in the new practice and known among the existing community before you officially start marketing for business in the new practice area. There are many possibilities and these jobs will change over time.

With the specific strategy in mind, you really want to build toward creating a LinkedIn presence that looks more like what you want to be and less like what you are right now. It's likely to be a gradual build, although there might be situations when you need to move quickly.

Next, map out your action steps in each of the three essential building blocks.

1. **Profile**. Start to emphasize your existing geographic connections or your experience (however limited) in the new practice area. For a new practice area, you might list each CLE seminar you attend in the new area. Add keywords to your About and Experience sections that are relevant to the new practice area or the clients in that area. If you are returning to the place you grew up, you probably will add your high school and other local information to your Profile. Over time, you will keep adding new items that relate to your move.

2. **Connections**. Prepare the ground. Add logical Connections as an active outreach project. Reach out to existing first degree Connections. Then start trying to convert relevant second-degree Connections to first-degree Connections. Searching for your first-degree and second-degree Connections in the new geographic area or practice area is the obvious first place to start. Alumni and former colleagues will be rich areas to mine. Look for thought leaders and opinion makers, as well as leadership of relevant organizations. What you would like to have is a strong, established network in advance of your move and a network that you can easily continue to build after your move. Having a well-thought-out Connection plan will pay dividends.

3. **Participation**. There is so much you can do in advance of your move. Join and participate in relevant LinkedIn Groups. Send Posts (links are good) that feature your desired geography or practice area. Follow thought leaders in the new area and engage with their content. LinkedIn Company pages are also a great place to find out competitive intelligence, practice information and job titles, and what's happening in a new community.

Consider your audience and use self-promotion sparingly, self-deprecatingly, and subtly. Always think about the actual value to others you bring and think about how you would react to someone else doing the same thing. There can be many creative approaches, but focus on providing helpful value to your target audience in your network.

Ultimately, your goal is to have a LinkedIn presence when you are ready to move that matches the presence of someone who is already there. Slow and steady wins the race. You might find many more opportunities and sooner than you expect. And, as you progress, take it to the real world. Work on getting phone calls, meetings for coffee or lunch, people to see on trips, and learning what is important in the new location or practice area.

26

USING LINKEDIN AS A BUSINESS

Although most of what we've discussed so far in this book centers around you as an individual, you can also use LinkedIn as a business or a law firm. In this Chapter, we'll cover several ways to use LinkedIn as a business—establishing a Company Page for your law firm or organization, creating Ads, Sponsored Posts or Targeted Posts, and using LinkedIn as a recruitment and hiring tool.

LinkedIn Company Pages

In addition to your own individual Profile, you (or a designated individual, such as a marketing director in a large law firm) can create a Company Page for your law firm or other organization.

All employees of your firm who have Profiles on LinkedIn will automatically be attached to your Company page, giving those employees' Profiles additional exposure. It is important for your employees to add their experience with your firm to their individual Profile with exactly the same spelling and in the same format as the Company Page to ensure that they are connected to the firm. For example, if the Company Page is listed under Smith Law LLC, but one of the firm's legal professionals adds the firm to their Profile as the Smith Law Firm, they will not properly connect to the Company Page.

Having a page for your firm on LinkedIn allows you to provide firm-wide information, not specific to any individual. You can expand your client base and demonstrate your firm's expertise even more through the use of Company pages and Company Updates. Think of it as a supplement to or an extension of your firm's or organization's website.

Creating Your Company Page

When creating your Company page, you will go through a process similar to creating your individual Profile. To get started, go to this page: ***https://business.linkedin.com/grow/building-your-brand*** and follow the steps to create your page. Or click the Work tab in the top navigation bar on any page in LinkedIn and scroll down to click "Create a Company Page".

You'll name the page, add a description, industry, location, header image, and logo, and designate administrators who can post Updates on the page on behalf of your firm. The recommended size for your logo is 300 x 300 pixels and the recommended size for your cover image is 1536 (w) x 768 (h) pixels. Your Company Page name is limited to 100 characters.

Elements of the Company Page

When LinkedIn users come to your Company Page, they will be directed to your Company **Home** page, where they will see your cover or header image, firm name, industry and location, a link to the firm website, and a chronological list of the Updates published on your Company Page. At the top of the Company Page, members will also be able to see how many of their Connections work at the firm or click on the link to see all employees of the firm.

Members can also click on **About** to see your firm's About page, which includes the firm's Overview or description, website link, and other basic information. Your Overview or About information must be between 200 and 1500 characters.

The **People** section of the Company Page shows members information about the employees of the company, including how many employees of the Company have LinkedIn Profiles, where they worked, what they studied, and how the member is connected to that Company.

Additional options are available if the Company Page has Career Pages enabled. (We'll discuss Career Pages later in this chapter).

Showcase Pages

Showcase Pages are sub-pages for LinkedIn Company Pages. Showcase Pages were introduced by LinkedIn in late 2013 as a way to highlight specific products or services, or to allow businesses to reach specific audiences who might be interested in only a segment of the company's offerings, rather than their general Company Page updates. For example, you might wish to create separate Showcase Pages for each of your practice areas under your main law firm LinkedIn Company Page.

Showcase pages can be especially helpful for law firms who have diverse practice areas and want to post different content to different audiences, because all of the Showcase Pages link back to the main Company Page and to one another.

You can create up to 10 Showcase Pages for each main LinkedIn Company Page, but you must be an administrator of the main Company Page to create a Showcase Page.

You can create a Showcase Page from the main navigation bar by clicking on Work and then "Create a Company Page" and then on "Showcase Page", or you can create the Showcase Page from the Admin tools dropdown on your existing Company Page.

Company Updates

On your Company page, you can post firm-wide Updates, events, and news. Once people find your Company page, they can follow your firm's news or Updates. Company Page Updates are limited to 700 characters, or 250 characters if the Update includes a link, which is plenty of room to provide summary information, links, and details about upcoming events.

Company Updates are seen on followers' Home pages in the Feed. Any LinkedIn user who visits your firm's Company Page can also see your Updates. Company Updates can be a great way to point people to specific pages on your website or items in your firm newsletter.

You can also ask followers to like, share, and comment on your updates so their network will see them and hopefully, visit your Page. We definitely recommend that you (1) encourage clients and others to follow your Company news and Updates and (2) include a link to (or the URL for) your Company page in email signatures, marketing materials, and other messaging.

Social Features

Any LinkedIn member can comment on, "like," or share a Company Update, the same way they would with an individual Update from a Connection, either in their Feed (if they follow the Company) or on the Company's Page. LinkedIn Company page administrators have the ability to choose whether to comment on, share or "like" Updates as the Company page, or as an individual LinkedIn member.

Targeted Updates

LinkedIn also allows Company Pages to post Targeted Updates, an option that is not available with individual Profiles. This is another way, in addition to Showcase Pages, to tailor content to a specific audience, particularly if you have multiple practice areas, although you pay for Targeted Updates, while Showcase Pages are free.

When you create an Update from your Company page, you can choose who you would like to share the post with, either Anyone or Targeted audience. Targeted company update filters are based on the user's profile data and include company size, industry, function, seniority, geography, and language preference. After selecting your criteria, you may choose to send your Update to employees and nonemployees or to nonemployees only.

To create a Targeted Update, draft the Update in your Company Page's admin panel and click "Public" from the privacy options. Then select "Targeted Audience" and define the parameters of your audience. Then click save and then post. LinkedIn will estimate the audience and give you a number of potential people who will see the Update. You can change audience filters to broaden or narrow the audience.

Targeted Updates are only seen by followers of the Company Page. Your firm must have at least three hundred followers of your Company Page to post a Targeted Update. Because Targeted Updates require your Company Page to have a large number of followers, and because those updates are limited to a subset of those followers, other paid options for targeting content might be more effective for most lawyers.

Sponsored Updates

Sponsored Updates are another way to broaden the reach of your Page on LinkedIn. They are another paid option that is only available to Company Pages, as opposed to individual Profiles. When you "sponsor" an update on your Company Page, you can specify a target audience for your update, and they will receive that update even if they are not following your Company Page. Sponsored Updates can be shared even further to Connections of a member who likes, comments, or shares the sponsored update. In this way, Sponsored Updates can help not only target your content to specific audiences, but also to reach outside of your own network or followers.

Sponsored Updates appear in the Home page Feed of LinkedIn members who fit the targeting criteria. You pay for sponsored updates based on the number of LinkedIn members who see the update, or the number of clicks the update receives.

If you're an administrator of the Company Page, you can sponsor a Company Page Update any time after you've posted it by creating a campaign to promote your update through the Campaign Manager. The content suggestions tab on the admin panel can help you find content that people are already engaging with. You can filter the suggestions to find content that might be most relevant to your audience. This is another way to curate content on LinkedIn to engage your audience without having to create your own content.

Company Page Analytics

As a Company page administrator, you have the ability not only to edit your page's contents but also to see analytics such as page views, unique visitors, and page clicks to track the effectiveness of your Company page, ads, and sponsored Updates. You will also be able to see specific insights about your Company's followers.

Driving Traffic to and Engagement with your LinkedIn Company Page

Just like real-world networking, the best way to get the most out of LinkedIn or any other 'community' or 'network' is to keep working it on a regular basis. Engage with others, including other legal professionals, strategic alliances, referral sources, and prospective clients. The same applies with your LinkedIn Company Page and Showcase Pages.

The first step is to make sure that all of your employees have LinkedIn Profiles and that they list the firm as their current employer. (As we said earlier, make sure they list it exactly the way it is listed on the firm's Company Page). When they do, they'll automatically become followers of the Company Page, and they'll show as employees of the firm when someone views the Company Page. If you've uploaded your logo to the Company Page, that logo will also show on the employees' Profiles, and it will be linked to your Company Page. This way, viewers of your employees' Profiles on LinkedIn will be directed to your Company Page if they click on the logo.

Next, create Updates both from your individual Profile and the Company Page, encouraging people to follow the page. Don't forget to mention the Company Page and following it in other marketing materials. Encourage (or incentivize) your employees to do the same. But keep in mind that when people land on your Page, they'll want to see information that is valuable to them, especially when they first visit the Company or Showcase Page. Otherwise, they won't have much incentive to click the "Follow" button.

Post Updates regularly and promote your Company page by adding a Follow button to your website or blog. Feature the Company page in e-mails, firm newsletters, and other marketing materials to encourage all of your audience to make it part of their LinkedIn experience. Be interesting. Be present. Help others—make introductions and connections, answer questions, and demonstrate your knowledge.

Unlike Facebook, there's no way within LinkedIn to send invitations to follow your Company page *per se*. You can send messages to your individual Connections personally asking them to follow your Page, and you can post Updates directing people to your Page or post about your Page in Groups and ask people to follow it (but beware of Group rules). However, LinkedIn is always making changes, so there may be some easier way in the future.

As more and more businesses begin using Company pages on LinkedIn, users will begin following these pages, just as they do on Facebook, Twitter, or other platforms. Given that LinkedIn is known as the professional network, however, followers of the Updates on your Company page are likely to be those interested in your practice or your professional associations.

LinkedIn has collected a lot of great information about Company pages in one place on its Frequently Asked Questions resource for Company pages at ***http://help.linkedin.com/app/answers/detail/a_id/1561***.

LinkedIn Ads

One more way to drive traffic to your content using LinkedIn, whether to your LinkedIn Page or to your website, products or services, is by using LinkedIn ads.

LinkedIn Ads allow you to create targeted advertisements to reach specific audiences. Since legal professionals frequently get referrals from other legal professionals, it's worth taking a look at how LinkedIn Ads work. You must have a LinkedIn account (basic or premium) to create advertisements through LinkedIn Ads.

The LinkedIn advertising product is fully self-service. You create the ads (text and image, text only, or video) yourself and pay online with a credit, debit, or other payment card. You can pay by the number of clicks or the number of impressions.

Creating a LinkedIn Ad Campaign

LinkedIn Ads can be found by clicking on Work in the main navigation menu, and then clicking "Advertise", which will take you to LinkedIn's Campaign Manager. LinkedIn uses a "wizard" approach to lead you through the ad creation, targeting, and payment process.

First, you'll design your ad campaign using the wizard. You'll give your campaign a name, create a headline and description, choose a language, add an image if you want, and preview your ad. You are limited to 25 characters for a text ad headline, and the body of the ad message is limited to 75 characters.

You can create and test up to 15 variations of the same ad to determine which approach is most successful. Take advantage of this tool. Even small changes in your ad can have a dramatic impact on results.

Second, you'll select a target audience for your ad. You can define the audience based on their industry, job function, title, or a host of other parameters.

Third, you will need to set a budget and bid on how much you're willing to pay for clicks or impressions. The minimum is $10/day, but you pay only for actual clicks or impressions, and there are no contracts or long-term commitments. You can stop your ad campaign at any time.

Finally, you'll check out and choose your payment option. That's all it takes to launch your LinkedIn ad campaign.

Tips for Creating LinkedIn Ads

LinkedIn Ads are similar to any other kind of advertising, so keep in mind:

- ► Target a specific audience.
- ► Use attention-getting language.
- ► Include a call to action.
- ► Direct the ads to a specific landing page, rather than to your firm's homepage, so you can track results.
- ► Track your traffic, clicks and conversions and tweak your ads if necessary.
- ► Include an image (maximum 50 pixels by 50 pixels) in your ad to create more interest. LinkedIn suggests that adding an image makes an ad 24% more effective than a text-only ad.
- ► LinkedIn recommends that you refresh your Ads at least monthly for best results.

LinkedIn collects helpful information about ads and shows examples on a Resources page at ***https://www.linkedin.com/ads/resources***. There is also a good Frequently Asked Questions page for LinkedIn Ads in the Help Center at ***http://help.linkedin.com/app/answers/detail/a_id/1015***.

If you are considering creating ads for your firm on LinkedIn, be sure to read LinkedIn's Ads Guidelines at ***https://www.linkedin.com/legal/pop/pop-sas-guidelines*** (and, of course, review your jurisdiction's ethical rules regarding advertising).

Using LinkedIn in the Hiring Process

As we discussed in Chapter 23, LinkedIn is often used as a job-seeking tool. For recruiters and employers, LinkedIn can be an ideal place to search for employment candidates. So how can you use LinkedIn to assist you when hiring new people?

If you have interviewed candidates recently, you might have already noticed the impact of LinkedIn on the hiring process. Well-prepared candidates seem to know more about your background than ever before. They might mention names of people that both you and they know. They might even say that they talked to a friend of yours who told them how great you are to work with. Although this can sometimes seem a little unsettling, it also leaves a favorable impression about the preparedness of the candidate. And it shows that the interviewee probably knows how to use LinkedIn.

Simply flip things around and you will see that you can do similar research when preparing to interview a candidate. The candidate's LinkedIn Profile might give you much more detailed information than a traditional one-page résumé and may be more informal and plainly written. If the candidate has Recommendations or Endorsements on their Profile, you might get a better picture of the candidate's capabilities or even learn that you know one of the recommenders or endorsers. The number of Endorsements a candidate has in certain Skills might give you a better picture of what the person does and what Skills others associate with the candidate, and you can compare the Skills the candidate has listed or has been endorsed for with the requirements of the position.

Best of all, you can check out what Connections you might share with a candidate so that you can talk about those relationships in the interview or even informally vet the candidate with a trusted Connection. Be aware, however, that some have expressed concern about the potential use of LinkedIn to find out information that might be illegal to ask about in interviews or to eliminate candidates on a discriminatory basis. All the laws and regulations (and company policies) that apply to what you do in the real world also apply to your use of LinkedIn in this context.

Posting a Job on LinkedIn

Many organizations routinely post job openings on LinkedIn. There are several ways to get to LinkedIn's Jobs wizard. You can click in the box to create a post from your LinkedIn Home page, and click "Share that you're hiring," or you can click on Jobs in the main navigation menu, and then click the button to post a job. Alternatively, you can click on Work in the main navigation menu and click on "Post a job" in the right column. The Jobs wizard will walk you through the process to provide detail for your job posting.

LinkedIn also has two premium accounts specifically for recruiters that might be helpful when you are hiring, as discussed in more detail in Chapter 26. Also, see the discussion of Career Pages below.

Here are some other ways to get the word out on LinkedIn about the job opening at your firm:

1. Post an Update indicating that your organization has a job opening and ask your Connections to put the word out to people who might be a good fit for your firm. Study the current research on how to word job postings in ways that encourage diversity candidates to apply and how to avoid pushing away good candidates.

2. Explore the Company page of the firm where a candidate currently works to get a better picture of what his or her work experience might really be and learn about the candidate's colleagues and supervisors.

3. View how the candidate has used the Skills component of LinkedIn and what Skills the candidate has highlighted. Compare them with what the candidate highlights in the interview (and what skills the job requires). You can also check the number of Endorsements a candidate has for the specific Skills that matter most to you.

4. Incorporate mentions of shared Connections into your interview questions.

5. Monitor Posts in your Feed for ideas about who might be interested in joining your firm or organization. Observe changes in firms or note a Connection who might be looking for a new job. You might notice that someone you thought was content in a position is actually looking for a job or might be receptive to your inquiry because others are leaving his or her firm. If you want to be aggressive, use LinkedIn to find prospects and assess their interest or ask them to recommend others who might fit your job description.

6. Read the Posts and other information the candidate makes public and view the Groups he or she has joined to gauge areas of interest.

Career Pages

Career Pages may be another way to attract potential candidates to your firm. Career Pages can only be created through a paid subscription, and they add additional sections to your Company Page—Jobs and either Life or What we Do, depending on the organization. The Life tab will display if the Company Page is for a company (e.g., your firm), university, college or high school, while Company Pages for search and staffing companies will instead display a What We Do tab.

The Jobs tab will display even without Career Pages enabled and a paid subscription, but without the upgrade, it will not show any Jobs, although it will allow LinkedIn users to create job alerts should your firm post a Job in the future. With a Career Page added to your Company Page, members will also see jobs recommended for them as well as employees who currently occupy the role.

According to LinkedIn, "The Life tab provides targeted audiences a personalized look into your organization, culture, and jobs through custom modules and unique insights." The Life/What we Do tab is essentially a glimpse inside your firm and your culture for recruiting and hiring purposes. LinkedIn provides several sections that can be customized to your firm and organization to showcase the firm's culture based on specific targeted parameters you provide.

Sections or modules that can be added include a main image or video, photos, employee perspectives, testimonials and leaders of the company. Different versions of the page can be shown to different target audiences based on information in the viewer's LinkedIn profile such as language, geography, job function, company size, industry, and seniority level.

Much as LinkedIn changed the job-seeking process, it has the potential to change the hiring and interviewing process as well.

A surprising number of companies are already using LinkedIn as the primary way they post job openings. There are great potential benefits, but, not surprisingly, LinkedIn raises some new hiring etiquette issues. Here is one interesting question: should you accept a candidate's invitation to connect during the interview process or extend your invitation to connect during the interview process? Watch as LinkedIn becomes part of the hiring process and observe ways that you can use the site to help you hire the best people.

LinkedIn Profinder

LinkedIn Profinder is a way that LinkedIn uses to match freelance professionals with those who need their services. It lists professionals by categories, one of which is legal. Profinder is a service that could potentially be of use to legal professionals in hiring designers, editors, or content strategists and the like, but it also could be a potential source of revenue or new clients.

As of this writing, we don't know any legal professionals who have used Profinder as a service provider and found success with it, but it might be worth checking out. You get 10 free proposals with Profinder, after which you'll need to register for a Premium Business account. But if Profinder brings you business, the cost will be far outweighed by fees received. While there is a cost to service providers, Profinder is free for those seeking to hire a service provider.

LinkedIn users can fill out a short form with some information about the service they are looking for, and that request goes out to those professionals on LinkedIn who have registered with Profinder for that service. The professional then sends a proposal in response to the request, and the requestor can choose to contact the professionals whose proposal(s) they like best.

To become a service provider with LinkedIn Profinder, you need to apply by clicking on the Work tab and choosing Profinder, then following the steps to apply. LinkedIn will create a Profinder Profile for you, pulling information from your personal Profile. Here again, it is important that your Headline matches what you list as your services on Profinder, and your About section, Skills, and Recommendations should all align with the types of work you are seeking.

You can learn more about LinkedIn Profinder here: ***https:// www.linkedin.com/profinder***.

Conclusion

As you can see, LinkedIn offers a number of services to help you gain visibility for and grow your business. Some of these options are free, but many more are paid. But even the paid options are flexible, allowing you to set budgets for ads and other sponsored campaigns, or to opt for a Premium Business account for a short period of time to gain access to Profinder requests as needed. We anticipate that LinkedIn will continue to expand its paid offerings and advertising opportunities for businesses or law firms that wish to avail themselves of these opportunities.

27

LINKEDIN FOR MILLENNIALS AND OTHERS NEW TO THE PLATFORM

By Grace Kennedy

"W hy are you using LinkedIn?" Young people, especially students and recent graduates, hear this question a lot when someone learns that they are on LinkedIn. It's a fair question.

Is it to find a new position, connect with other people in your field, or to follow companies that you purchase from or are interested in? Is it to showcase your resume and skill set? Or, is it simply because someone else told you to?

With these questions in mind, I've compiled a short list of my favorite tips for building your LinkedIn profile to assist you in finding meaningful work and employers who will value you and your skill set.

When I joined LinkedIn in 2014, I was a college student working as a waitress while I finished undergrad. I didn't have a desire to get another job because I was making the money I needed to afford my rent and keep up with my classwork and grades. So, I kept my profile idle and my activity at a minimum.

However, once I graduated from college, I noticed the great potential LinkedIn could have on my job search and ability to connect with other professionals. Without LinkedIn, I would not have this opportunity at my fingertips.

I've worked on my LinkedIn presence steadily since then. I can trace jobs and opportunities directly to relationships started on LinkedIn. Without LinkedIn, I would not have had the chance to help plan and conduct a legal design thinking unconference, meet other like-minded professionals, and market my myself and my skill set. I am building my own professional network with the help of LinkedIn.

But, enough about me. I want to share with you some of my favorite tips for building your LinkedIn profile, especially when you are a student or a recent graduate and might be wondering whether using LinkedIn makes any sense for you. My goal is to help you find meaningful work and employers who will value you and your skill set and also find customers and partners for your side gigs. Shine on!

1. Just a Sample.

Your LinkedIn is a sample of what you can do, not the whole package.

Your LinkedIn should make people curious about you. It should excite employers and inspire people to contact you. But it is only one part of you: the virtual part. It is the sample for people to try, and if they like what they see, they can contact you to find out more. Leave a little for the imagination!

2. Privacy matters.

While LinkedIn is marketed for professional use, this does not mean that everyone follows the guidelines. There have been reports from users about experiencing harassment from past relationships or partners, especially people of my age, both female and male, especially in the LGBTQ+ community. If you are concerned about your safety and privacy, one tip I recommend is not to list or identify your current workplace. Instead, list only your prior work experience that you are comfortable with the entire world knowing. Because it doesn't matter how ironclad you think your privacy settings are, this is the Internet and stalkers will stalk. Treat every word you put out there as something for the entire world to see.

3. Authenticity is meaningful.

Don't discount your profile because you don't have a list of "great" jobs or be embarrassed because you have fewer than 100 connections. I've read many articles about the "importance" of having 500+ connections. I'd like to challenge that by saying it's not how many connections you have, but rather how your connections speak to your breadth of experience. If you have certain job or volunteer experience listed on your profile, you'll be much more likely to generate interest if your connections showcase that you built genuine rapport at your workplace.

Anyone can buy 5,000 followers for just $199 now, so it's about why you choose to connect, not your numbers.

4. Make Your Own Rules.

Challenge what you read, even in this book, or what you've heard LinkedIn is "supposed" to be. Do your homework, decide what's best for all and make your own decisions. There is no magic formula. Your LinkedIn presence is yours for the making. So, get creative and share your voice like only YOU can!

Inspired? Get going! You've got work to do.

I'm using LinkedIn as a point of contact for project commissions and job offers, as a way to connect with employers, colleagues, and past mentors, and finally, as a platform that allows me to market myself and what I can offer to others.

What will you use it for?

28

LINKEDIN AND LEGAL ETHICS

E ven though LinkedIn is geared toward professional, as opposed to social, interaction, there are still ways that lawyers can run afoul of the ethical rules in their jurisdiction if they are not careful.

All lawyers should be familiar with the ethical rules in their jurisdiction, including rules as they relate to advertising, solicitation, and communication about the lawyer or law firm's services. But many lawyers seem to forget these rules when engaging in online activities or don't apply them appropriately. Some of these ethical breaches occur inadvertently, or as a result of headings or settings that the lawyer or law firm has no control over because they are set by the platform itself. But the mere fact that the lawyer cannot control the setting doesn't necessarily mean that the lawyer is safe, as several ethics opinions have established.

We encourage all lawyers to regularly review the ethical rules and recent ethics opinions in their jurisdictions, especially because many jurisdictions are actively revising their rules to specifically cover online advertising and social media, or are issuing opinions specifically directed to lawyers' use of social media, including LinkedIn. The good news is that, for the most part, the history of lawyers and other legal professionals using LinkedIn over the years has been the story of good judgment and appropriate use. This history has largely given regulators a degree of comfort with LinkedIn that they don't have with other social media tools and blogging.

In this section we will refer to the ABA Model Rules to cover some of the main ethical issues that might arise with lawyers' use of LinkedIn, along with some examples from opinions in different jurisdictions, but many states have different (and stricter) rules, so it is important that you become familiar with your own state's rules and the opinions interpreting them. And, of course, we disclaim that we are giving any legal advice.

This book focuses on the use of LinkedIn as a marketing and business development tool, but there are also ethical and legal issues lawyers must be aware of when using LinkedIn as an investigative tool for litigation or in the hiring process, and some of those opinions are listed in the Resources section of this book for your reference.

False or Misleading Information

As a general rule, lawyers are prohibited from making false or misleading statements about themselves or their services as indicated in ABA Model Rule 7.1.

To avoid being misleading, a lawyer or law firm must keep any online presence, including a LinkedIn Profile, up-to-date and ensure that disclaimers prevent website visitors from developing unjustified expectations (see Disclaimers, below). Outdated or inaccurate information should be removed.

For example, New York State Bar Association Committee on Professional Ethics Opinion 1005, dated April 2, 2014, found that neither the statement, "I know how to win for you" nor "unsurpassed litigation skills" in lawyer advertising is permissible under New York's version of Rule 7.1 because the statements are misleading, and neither statement could be factually supported as of the date on which it was disseminated. Similar cases in other jurisdictions have yielded similar opinions. Keep in mind that this language would have been a problem no matter what media it was used in.

For lawyers who post or link to articles on substantive law on their LinkedIn Profiles, it may be wise to date the post or article and include a notice that the legal information was accurate as of the date of the writing, that the law changes frequently, and that readers should not rely solely on the online information but should consult a lawyer who can discuss their specific situation. However, there is a growing awareness that information on the Internet can change and must be read critically and verified independently.

Lawyers should also use care in the way they present information on their LinkedIn Profile to make it clear where they are admitted to practice law, so that they avoid the fate of one lawyer who was disciplined after it was discovered that his LinkedIn Profile implied that he was admitted to practice law in Pennsylvania when in fact he was only admitted in Colorado.

The prohibition against the use of false or misleading statements also implicates other rules of professional conduct which may come into play in the use of LinkedIn, including Model Rule 4.1 (Truthfulness in Statements to Others); Model Rule 4.3 (Dealing with Unrepresented Persons); Model Rule 4.4 (Respect for Rights of Third Persons); Model Rule 7.1 (Communications About Lawyers Services); Model Rule 7.4 (Communication of Fields of Practice and Specialization) and Model rule 8.4 (Misconduct).

Lawyers must use caution when interacting with unrepresented third parties online or when using social media as a means to obtain information about a party or adversary. Generally, any information that is publicly available is considered fair game, but things get a bit more complicated when information is protected by an individual's privacy settings. Using trickery or false statements to obtain information can be problematic, as, of course, it can be in the non-LinkedIn world.

Confidentiality

Client confidentiality is one of the cornerstones of legal practice, and there are several ways the ethics rules related to client confidentiality can come into play when using LinkedIn.

Posting about client matters

ABA Model Rules 1.6 and 1.9 govern confidentiality and prohibit lawyers from revealing information relating to the representation of a client unless the client gives informed consent.

Posting about ongoing client matters in individual Posts or within Groups—even without mentioning a client by name—can be problematic. In fact, posting about "live" cases and matters might be the hottest area in legal ethics today.

In 2018, the ABA Standing Committee on Professional Responsibility released Formal Opinion 480, Confidentiality Obligations for Lawyer Blogging and Other Public Commentary, reminding lawyers that their duties of confidentiality extend to blogging and other online activities.

The opinion cautions lawyers about commenting publicly about cases or information relating to the representation of a client, including the fact of representation, *even if some of that information is already publicly available*.

There are exceptions to these rules which would allow a lawyer to publicly comment on the representation of a client, including the "generally known" exception under Rule 1.9.

Many lawyers may have thought that they were free to comment on cases if they were a matter of public record, such as where a decision or verdict could be easily accessed by a jury verdict search or by obtaining the court file. But the opinion reminds lawyers that the confidentiality rule is much broader than attorney-client privilege and that it applies to more than just communication between the lawyer and the client.

The confidentiality rules cover all information relating to the representation, regardless of the information's origin. Citing ABA Formal Opinion 479, The "Generally Known" Exception to Former-Client Confidentiality, issued in December 2017, Opinion 480 cautions lawyers that even if information can be found in a public record, such as a court decision, it is still subject to the duty of confidentiality.

Opinion 479 clarifies the "generally known" exception to the duty of confidentiality under Rule 1.9, stating that the exception applies to the use, and not the revelation of client information, and then it applies,

> *...only if the information has become (a) widely recognized by members of the public in the relevant geographic area; or (b) widely recognized in the former client's industry, profession, or trade.*

> *Information is not "generally known" simply because it has been discussed in open court, or is available in court records, in libraries, or in other public repositories of information.*

The New York Bar Association Committee on Professional Ethics issued a similar opinion in June 2017, Opinion 1125 ,(cited in Opinion 479) which states that, "Although information that is generally known in the local community is not protected as confidential information, information is not 'generally known' simply because it is in the public domain or available in a public file."

Another New York opinion cited by ABA 479, Opinion, 991 (2013) notes that, "information is generally known only if it is known to a sizeable percentage of people in 'the local community or in the trade, field or profession to which the information relates.'"

According to Opinion 479, "Unless information has become widely recognized by the public (for example by having achieved public notoriety), or within the former client's industry, profession, or trade, the fact that the information may have been discussed in open court, or may be available in court records, in public libraries, or in other public repositories does not, standing alone, mean that the information is generally known for Model Rule 1.9(c)(1) purposes."

In short, these opinions distinguish between publicly available information and information that would qualify as "generally known." There must be some showing beyond the fact that the information is a matter of public record to qualify for the exception.

How do these opinions affect lawyers using LinkedIn? Both Rule 1.6 and Rule 1.9 permit the revelation of client information with the consent of the client. (There are other exceptions as well, but they do not apply in the context of LinkedIn). The best way for lawyers to protect themselves and ensure compliance with ethics rules is to obtain written consent from the client before posting or commenting about their matter on LinkedIn. It might be best to write it, get it out of your system, let it rest for a few days, and then decide whether it is important enough to ask your client for permission to post it. You'll feel better and will avoid all the potential difficulties a hasty and angry post can cause.

Lawyers are always free to comment generally on legal issues and could certainly blog about issues they have encountered in various cases. They can also use hypotheticals, point to cases from the news, or comment on reported decisions to illustrate legal concepts.

When using hypotheticals based on their own cases, lawyers should heed the warnings contained in these various ethics opinions and ensure that there is no reasonable likelihood that a third party could ascertain the client's identity from the way the hypothetical is described.

Finally, even lists of clients contained on a lawyer's LinkedIn Profile would be covered by the confidentiality rules, so lawyers whose Profiles contain these kinds of lists should ensure that they have documentation of the clients' consent to do so.

Communicating through LinkedIn

Communications through LinkedIn (Messages, inMail, and invitations to connect) can also raise confidentiality issues, and lawyers should take care to ensure that the confidentiality of communications with prospective clients is preserved when responding to questions or messages on LinkedIn. Lawyers should provide only general responses and should caution those asking questions on LinkedIn, whether in Groups or even through private Messages, that confidentiality cannot be expected and that further communication should take place off-line.

ABA Formal Opinion 477R (2017) provides some guidance on the steps lawyers should take to protect client information transmitted over the Internet, and Model Rule 1.6(c) specifically addresses a lawyer's obligation to take reasonable measures to prevent inadvertent or unauthorized disclosure of information relating to a lawyer's representation of a client.

Connecting with clients on LinkedIn

Lawyers often ask us whether connecting to current clients raises some confidentiality issues, particularly for clients with sensitive legal matters such as bankruptcy or divorce. But the risk appears to be low, since you cannot connect with someone on LinkedIn without their consent (they must accept your invitation to connect or send you an invitation themselves). In addition, it is unclear whether anyone looking at your LinkedIn Profile or your Connections would know that the individual was a client, as opposed to a neighbor, friend, colleague, or coworker. But these decisions must be made on a case-by-case basis, and you should be aware of potential confidentiality issues when requesting or accepting LinkedIn invitations from clients.

Advertising

Most jurisdictions have special rules governing lawyer advertising. Is your LinkedIn Profile considered advertising? In many jurisdictions, the answer is yes. In August 2010, the ABA issued Formal Opinion 10-457, an ethics opinion about lawyer websites, which provides that if online activities promote a law practice, they are considered lawyer advertising. That means that if your LinkedIn Profile (or Company page) promotes you as a lawyer, it would be considered an advertisement and must comply with the advertising rules. Is a LinkedIn Profile simply informational or is it promotional? Reasonable minds can reach different conclusions, as can be seen in the two different approaches taken by two New York bar associations, the New York City Bar Association, in Opinion 2015-7and the New York County Lawyers Association, in Opinion 748, both issued in 2015.

Opinion 2015-7, Application of Attorney Advertising Rules to LinkedIn, said, in part, that,

> To constitute advertising, the LinkedIn content must meet all five of the following criteria: (a) it must be made by or on behalf of the lawyer; (b) its primary purpose must be for the retention of the lawyer by new clients for pecuniary gain; (b) the LinkedIn content must relate to the legal services offered by the lawyer; (c) its intended audience must be potential new clients; and (d) the LinkedIn content must not fall within a recognized exception or exclusion to the definition of attorney advertising.

In contrast, Opinion 748 said that an attorney's LinkedIn presence which contains anything more than a mere listing of barebones information about a lawyer's experience and education on LinkedIn would constitute advertising.

The Florida Supreme Court overhauled its lawyer advertising rules in 2013, making it clear that websites and social media sites are subject to the same restrictions as more traditional forms of advertising, and California Ethics Opinion 2012-186 concluded that the lawyer advertising rules in that state applied to social media posts, depending on the nature of the posted statement or content. It is reasonable to believe that even states that haven't stated so directly will apply the same rules to social media if they have not promulgated specific rules about social media use.

ABA Model Rule 7.2(c) requires any communication considered advertising to include the name and office address of at least one lawyer or law firm responsible for its content. If your jurisdiction's rule is similar, be sure that your firm's office address appears somewhere in your LinkedIn Profile.

Some states require prior review of advertisements or solicitations (for more on solicitations, see below), giving rise to questions about whether your LinkedIn Profile could be posted or substantially updated, or whether embedded videos or presentations could be posted, without prior review. For example, under the Texas Disciplinary Rules for Professional Conduct, Rule 7.07 says that law firm advertising must be submitted to the Advertising Review Committee of the state bar. It has been determined that law firm or individual lawyer videos uploaded to sites like YouTube and Facebook must be submitted for review. It is unclear whether regular social networking updates must also be submitted. Texas seems to have clarified that certain social media sites, such as LinkedIn, do not; but you must, of course, confirm that for yourself and your jurisdiction.

Solicitation

Many states have special rules concerning solicitation, separate and apart from the general rules governing lawyer advertising. Generally, solicitation is distinguished from advertising because it involves direct contact with a specific person (or group of people) for the purpose of getting hired, rather than an advertisement sent or available to the general public. Individual requests to connect or direct messages through LinkedIn's InMail service might be considered solicitations in some circumstances.

In 2010, the Philadelphia Bar Association issued an opinion (Philadelphia Bar Assn. Profl. Guidance Comm., Op. 2010-6) that its Rule 7.3 does not bar lawyers from using social media for solicitation where the prospective client has the ability to ignore the soliciting lawyer. Given that those receiving messages or invitations to connect on LinkedIn can ignore the request and simply not respond, this opinion might be read to permit lawyers to solicit using LinkedIn—at least in Philadelphia.

ABA Model Rule 7.3 governs direct contact with prospective clients. Subsection (a) prohibits "real-time electronic contact [to] solicit professional employment from a prospective client when a significant motive for the lawyer's doing so is the lawyer's pecuniary gain," with specific exceptions. Subsection (c) requires any such communication to include a disclaimer (see Disclaimers, below).

Disclaimers

ABA Model Rule 7.3(c) requires that every electronic communication from a lawyer soliciting professional employment from a prospective client known to be in need of legal services in a particular matter include the words "advertising material," unless it falls under one of the exceptions listed in Rule 7.3. Many jurisdictions not only share this requirement but also have even stricter rules requiring disclaimers in broader circumstances.

Whether your jurisdiction requires it or not, it is wise to include some kind of disclaimer on your LinkedIn Profile indicating that visiting your Profile, viewing presentations or other content, or contacting you through LinkedIn does not establish a lawyer-client relationship and that this contact might not be confidential. Make sure your disclaimers are clear and easy to understand.

Since there is no obvious place to add disclaimers to your Profile, we recommend that you add them to your About or Experience sections. If your firm has a Company page, you will likely want to add disclaimers to your Page's Overview section as well.

You may also need to add disclaimers when discussing legal issues online, such as in Group discussions on LinkedIn, even when those discussions are general in nature. Keep in mind that LinkedIn is a global platform, so many of those reading what you post on LinkedIn will be outside of your jurisdiction.

Specialization and "Expert" Status

Although lawyers are permitted to communicate the areas of law in which they practice, many jurisdictions prohibit lawyers from proclaiming that they are "specialists" or "experts" in any particular field, absent certification by an approved, accredited authority. ABA Model Rule 7.4 also requires that the name of the accrediting organization be clearly identified.

LinkedIn has removed the Specialties section from the Profile template for anyone who creates a new Profile, but users who filled in this section when it was available will still see this section displayed on their Profile at the end of the About section. Including this section could be problematic, and many lawyers have removed it.

If your firm has a LinkedIn Company page, there is still a "Specialties" section at the bottom of the Overview. Unless *all* lawyers in the firm are certified in any of the areas the firm wishes to list, it may be wise to simply leave this section blank. New York State Bar Association Committee on Professional Ethics released Opinion 972 in June of 2013 which specifically advises that law firms **should not** list specialties on their LinkedIn Company Page. The opinion notes that while firms are permitted to list their areas of practice, they may not do so under a "Specialties" heading, even where (as here) the firm has no control over the heading and cannot change it. The rule not only prohibits individual lawyers from claiming a "specialty," but law firms cannot use the term either.

As a practical matter, this restriction should not create too many problems for purposes of creating an effective law firm Company Page, as firms can simply list the practice areas in the general firm description, and can list them separately as individual Showcase Pages (which are sub-pages to the main Company Page).

In some jurisdictions, the ethics rules might also make filling in the Skills section on your Profile difficult if you are not certified in a particular specialty, although at least one jurisdiction has indicated that adding practice areas to this section is not a violation (see Resources). This problem has also largely been solved now that LinkedIn has changed this section's title from "Skills and Expertise" to "Skills and Endorsements." Even so, some lawyers have addressed this prohibition by putting a disclaimer in the About section noting that the designated skills are not meant to imply certification in a particular specialty.

Inadvertent Lawyer-Client Relationship and Un-authorized Practice of Law

As noted above, answering questions, participating in discussions and posting updates on LinkedIn necessarily exposes your message to those outside the jurisdiction in which you practice. As such, you must be mindful of ABA Model Rule 5.5, which prohibits the unauthorized practice of law or practice outside of a jurisdiction in which you are admitted to practice, subject to certain exceptions. Don't forget that whether the client relationship exists is determined from the client's perspective, not yours.

You should also use caution when answering questions in discussions or Groups on LinkedIn, just as you would on sites such as Avvo, JD Supra, Quora, or similar services, to make sure that you are not creating an inadvertent lawyer-client relationship or offering legal advice. ABA Formal Opinion 10-457 cites several cases from a variety of states noting that because lawyers cannot screen for conflicts of interest when answering questions posted on the Internet, they should refrain from answering specific legal questions unless the advice given is not fact-specific. However, it should be noted that many jurisdictions do permit lawyers to answer hypothetical questions.

Additionally, in determining if a lawyer-client relationship has been established or if a lawyer has violated the prohibition against unauthorized practice of law, the rules and opinions place a great deal of importance on who controls the flow of information and whether that information is provided unilaterally or is part of a bilateral discussion, as well as the subsequent actions of the lawyer or firm once the communication is received (see ABA Formal Opinion 10-457 and ABA Model Rule 1.18).

Recommendations and Endorsements

Some jurisdictions prohibit testimonials or recommendations entirely, whereas others allow them from former, but not current, clients. Still others permit all testimonials. Most jurisdictions require some kind of disclaimer to accompany these testimonials. If this is the case in your jurisdiction, you might need to provide those who recommend you on LinkedIn with disclaimer language to place at the bottom of their Recommendation.

To make these issues even more complicated, some states differentiate between "testimonials" and "endorsements." As we discussed in Chapter 16, LinkedIn permits both long-form Recommendations and one-click Endorsements, so be sure to find out how your jurisdiction handles different kinds of client comments.

Be aware of the Skills your clients endorse you for; they may not be Skills with which you are comfortable. You may also want to be careful accepting Endorsements from those whom you do not believe have actual knowledge of your Skills. While LinkedIn has ended the practice of allowing your Connections to endorse you for "new" Skills that you did not add to your Profile, you will want to review your Skills and Endorsements to ensure that they are accurate, and to reject or remove inappropriate Endorsements from your Profile.

Even if your jurisdiction permits you to accept endorsements and/or recommendations, do not engage in the practice of reciprocal endorsements. Just because someone recommends or endorses you doesn't mean you need to reciprocate. Reciprocal recommendations can be seen as a violation of ABA Model Rule 7.2, which prohibits lawyers from giving anything of value in exchange for a recommendation.

Lawyers are responsible not only for what they publish on the Internet about themselves but also for what others publish about them. Although Recommendations can be great for your practice, you must diligently review them to ensure that your clients are not using terms that are prohibited by your jurisdiction's ethical rules. The general standard is that you can make claims that can be objectively proved. Phrases like "best tax lawyer in America" or "most awesome real estate lawyer ever" would not meet that standard. You must also be sure that the Recommendation cannot be considered false or misleading. Remember that you can (and should!) approve and manage the Recommendations you receive before they are posted.

According to New York County Lawyers Association Opinion 748, "The ethical treatment of endorsements and recommendations depends on who is considered to "own" the endorsement and recommendation: the author of the endorsement or recommendation or the person whose profile is enhanced by it."

On LinkedIn, users have control over what is posted on their own Profiles. They can choose to reject or hide an Endorsement, and Recommendations do not appear on a user's Profile unless approved by the owner of the Profile. Accordingly, Opinion 748 holds lawyers responsible for ensuring the accuracy of what appears on their Profiles, stating that, "there is a duty to review social networking sites and confirm their accuracy periodically, at reasonable intervals." Again, this may differ depending on your jurisdiction.

Technology Competence

ABA Model Rule 1.1 states that "A lawyer shall provide competent representation to a client. Competent representation requires the legal knowledge, skill, thoroughness and preparation reasonably necessary for the representation." Comment 8 to this rule adds the clarification: "To maintain the requisite knowledge and skill, a lawyer *should keep abreast of changes in the law and its practice, including the benefits and risks associated with relevant technology*, engage in continuing study and education and comply with all continuing legal education requirements to which the lawyer is subject." [emphasis added] The words about relevant technology were added to the comment in 2012 and, at the time this book was published, thirty-six states had adopted this language.

Many people now refer to this as the "technology competence requirement." The requirement is to "keep abreast of changes" in "relevant technology." It is possible to do full-hour continuing legal education programs on technology competence (and both of us have done so). However, we will make just a few points about LinkedIn.

The core question under Comment 8 is: "Is LinkedIn a 'relevant technology' for which a lawyer should keep abreast of changes in the law or its practice?" It's difficult to argue, at this point, that LinkedIn is not relevant to the practice of law, for the many reasons we have discussed in this book. LinkedIn has also become an essential tool for obtaining biographical backgrounds on opposing counsel, expert witnesses, and many others, and for mapping the web of their Connections. In some matters, analyzing LinkedIn usage might also be important in cross-examination or establishing damages in an employment case.

To be fair, as of the time this book was published, we have not been able to find any instances where a lawyer was publicly reprimanded or otherwise disciplined for the failure to meet the technology competence requirement (although failures to understand and use technology might have played a role in other issues, such as missed deadlines or failure to communicate). In fact, the practical risk that a lawyer will be disbarred or suspended for failing to meet the technology competence requirement with respect to LinkedIn is quite low. The greater risk with LinkedIn is in some of the other areas highlighted above. The bigger concerns will be in malpractice risk, when a client believes that a lawyer missed important facts available by LinkedIn and in the general risk of losing clients and becoming irrelevant or invisible because you are not perceived to exist in a meaningful way on LinkedIn.

Ethics Tips

The best rule of thumb when considering what you can and cannot do on LinkedIn (or any other social networking site) is to not say anything that you would not be comfortable saying or doing in a roomful of people or publishing on the front page of *The Wall Street Journal*. A corollary would be to exercise extreme caution in saying anything about the details of a current case or matter. Even better, avoid commenting on current cases altogether, and obtain client consent in writing before sharing about a closed matter.

Make sure you have a social media policy for your law firm that clearly spells out the firm's guidelines for use of social media by everyone in the office.

Watch out for specialized issues that arise out of social media usage. For example, the use of social media by and with judges has already raised a number of questions. Become familiar with the ethical rules in your jurisdiction about friending judges on Facebook or connecting with them on LinkedIn and other social media. Fortunately, jurisdictions (and judges themselves) are more open than ever to the professional use of LinkedIn, Twitter, and other social media and the guidance for judges is much clearer than it was in the past. This result is a good one, especially in the case where you have a good friend or law school classmate who becomes a judge. In that scenario, it's so much better to send them congratulations on LinkedIn rather than be forced to drop them as a Connection.

If you are litigator, you must learn and follow the rules for using social media as tool for investigating potential jurors, witnesses, and opposing parties. A good starting point for coverage of ethics opinions on this topic is "Legal Ethics Opinions Related to Attorneys' Use of Social Media Profiles for Investigative and Background Research (***https://www.netforlawyers.com/content/legal-ethics-opinions-lawyers-attorneys-social-media-investigative-background-research-0045***).

Final Thoughts

In many ways, behavior on LinkedIn and social media is identical, at least conceptually, to behavior in the physical world, and the same ethical principles apply. When considering activities on LinkedIn, think about the ethical implications of comparable real-world activities. If you take that approach, being mindful of the basic principle of avoiding misrepresentation and staying aware of your state's specific rules or guidelines, you should be in good shape on the ethical front.

In the next chapter we have listed a number of important ethics opinions, some of which were referenced in this Chapter, but always keep in mind that social media is constantly evolving, and we expect ethical regulations will continue to evolve as regulators better understand social media tools. In fact, as this book is being published, we know of several jurisdictions seeking to further update amend their rules of professional responsibility to take into account changes in technology, including social media, as well as some that are seeking to create guidelines for attorneys on social media use. As in the real world, you must keep abreast of current developments.

In summary:

- ► Regulation of social media, including LinkedIn, is an evolving topic and you must keep abreast of developments

- ► Know and understand the opinions and approaches of the applicable jurisdictions for you and your practice

- ► Follow the core principle of avoiding the dissemination of misleading information

- ► Use appropriate and applicable disclaimers required in your jurisdiction(s)

- ► Have a solid understanding of the advertising and solicitation rules, including those about "expertise," testimonials, recommendations, and endorsements

- ► Realize that real-world ethics principles still apply on the Internet

- ► Implement a social media policy or add coverage of social media to existing firm policies

29

RESOURCES

General—Networking and LinkedIn

Dig Your Well Before You're Thirsty: The Only Networking Book You'll Ever Need, Harvey Mackey (Currency Books 1999).

Linked: How Everything Is Connected to Everything Else and What It Means for Business, Science, and Everyday Life, Albert-Laszlo Barabasi (Basic Books 2014).

Video: LinkedIn for Lawyers: Interview with Allison Shields, My Case Blog, *https://www.mycase.com/blog/2016/08/interview-allison-shields-linkedin-lawyers/*

Simple Steps: Developing a Basic Marketing Plan, Allison Shields, Law Practice Today, *https://www.americanbar.org/groups/law_practice/publications/law_practice_magazine/2019/MA2019/MA2019SimpleSteps/*

The Power Formula for LinkedIn Success (Fourth Edition—Completely Revised): Kick-start Your Business, Brand, and Job Search, Wayne Breitbarth (Greenleaf Book Group Press 2019).

LinkedIn for Dummies, Joe Elad (For Dummies 2018)

LinkedIn Help Center—*https://www.linkedin.com/help/linkedin*.

LinkedIn Marketing Techniques for Law and Professional Practices, Marc W. Halpert (American Bar Association 2017)

LinkedIn Unlocked: Unlock the Mystery of LinkedIn to Drive More Sales Through Social Selling, Melonie Dodaro (CreateSpace Independent Publishing Platform 2018)

Official LinkedIn Blog—*http://blog.linkedin.com/*.

Profile

5 LinkedIn Profile Mistakes Lawyers Make, Allison C. Shields, *https://www.linkedin.com/pulse/20140418203834-20898262-5-linkedin-profile-mistakes-lawyers-make/*

Do Something! Power Up Your LinkedIn Headline, Allison C. Shields, Legal Ease Blog, *https://www.legaleaseconsulting.com/legal_ease_blog/2018/02/do-something-power-up-your-linkedin-headline.html*

Video: How to Network on LinkedIn, Allison C. Shields, *https://www.youtube.com/watch?v=u2Ucq6Jgov0*

Video: Upgrade Your LinkedIn Headline, Allison C. Shields, *https://youtu.be/aTMVSaSURtY*

Webinar: Power Up Your LinkedIn Profile (Dennis Kennedy and Allison Shields)—*https://www.americanbar.org/careercenter/career-development-series/power-up-your-linkedin-profile/*

Connections

Podcast: "The 2018 LinkedIn Connection Competition," The Kennedy-Mighell Report Podcast—*https://legaltalknetwork.com/ podcasts/kennedy-mighell-report/2018/04/the-2018-linkedin- connection-competition/*

Podcast: "The 2018 LinkedIn Connection Competition Results," The Kennedy-Mighell Report Podcast—*https://legaltalknetwork.com/ podcasts/kennedy-mighell-report/2018/06/the-2018-linkedin- connection-competition-results/*

Six Ways to Jump Start Your LinkedIn Network, Dennis Kennedy & Allison Shields—*https://www.lawtechnologytoday.org/2016/09/ six-ways-to-jump-start-your-linkedin-network/*

Participation

Tips on Using LinkedIn Groups, Allison C. Shields, *https://www.linkedin.com/pulse/20140613201718- 20898262-tips-on-using-linkedin-groups/*

Ethics

American Bar Association and the Center for Professional Responsibility. Model Rules of Professional Conduct, 2013 Edition. Chicago: American Bar Association, 2013. *http:// www.americanbar.org/groups/professional_responsibility/ publications/model_rules_of_professional_conduct/model_rules_ of_professional_conduct_table_of_contents.html.**

Social Media Ethics Guidelines of the Commercial and Federal Litigation Sections of the New York State Bar Association (Updated June 9, 2015), *http://www.nysba.org/socialmediaguidelines/*

DC Bar Ethics Opinion 370, Social Media I: Use of Social Media for Personal Use, November 2016, *https://www.dcbar.org/bar-resources/legal-ethics/opinions/Ethics-Opinion-370.cfm*

DC Bar Ethics Opinion 371, Social Media II: Use of Social Media in Providing Legal Services, November 2016, *https://www.dcbar.org/bar-resources/legal-ethics/opinions/Ethics-Opinion-371.cfm*

New York City Bar Ethics Opinion 2015-7: Application of Attorney Advertising Rules to LinkedIn, *https://www.nycla.org/siteFiles/Publications/Publications1748_0.pdf*

New York County Lawyers' Association Opinion 748 (2015): Ethical Implications of Attorney Profiles on LinkedIn, *https://www.nycbar.org/member-and-career-services/committees/reports-listing/reports/detail/formal-opinion-2015-7-application-of-attorney-advertising-rules-to-linkedin*

Colorado Bar Association Opinion 127 Use of Social Media for Investigative Purposes, September 2015, *http://www.cobar.org/Portals/COBAR/repository/ethicsOpinions/FormalEthicsOpinion_127.pdf*

Ariz. Judicial Ethics Op. 14-01 (2014), use of social and electronic media by judges and judicial employees

Pa. Ethics Op. 2014-300

N.C. Ethics Op. 8 (2012)

ABA Formal Opinion 466: Lawyers Reviewing Jurors' Internet Presence *https://www.americanbar.org/content/dam/aba/ administrative/professional_responsibility/formal_opinion_466_ final_04_23_14.authcheckdam.pdf*

New York County Lawyers Association Formal Opinion 743 (2011) Lawyer investigation of juror internet and social networking postings during conduct of trial. *https://www.nycla.org/siteFiles/ Publications/Publications1450_0.pdf*

West Virginia Disciplinary Opinion 2015-02, Social Media and Attorneys, September 2015 *http://www.wvodc.org/pdf/LEO%20 2015%20-%2002.pdf*

Oregon Opinion 2013-189 Accessing Information About Third-Parties Through a Social Networking Website, February 2013 *https://www.osbar.org/_docs/ethics/2013-189.pdf*

Association of the Bar of the City of New York, Formal Opinion 2012-2, Jury Research and Social Media, May 30, 2012 *http://www. nycbar.org/member-and-career-services/committees/reports-listing/reports/detail/formal-opinion-2012-2-jury-research-and-social-media*

ABA Formal Opinion 466, Lawyer Reviewing Jurors' Internet Presence, April 24, 2014, *http://www.americanbar.org/content/ dam/aba/administrative/professional_responsibility/formal_ opinion_466_final_04_23_14.authcheckdam.pdf*

New York State Bar Association Committee on Professional Ethics Opinion 972 *http://www.nysba.org/CustomTemplates/Content. aspx?id=28101*

30

WHEN YOU NEED HELP

Although all of the techniques and strategies we've laid out in this book are relatively straightforward, that doesn't mean that they are all easy or quick to implement. Using LinkedIn well takes time and the discipline to consistently engage, as well as to keep up with the frequent changes LinkedIn makes to the platform.

It becomes even more difficult if you're a managing partner, marketing director or department head who is in charge of ensuring that all of the legal professionals in your department or employees at the firm not only create a LinkedIn Profile, but that they keep those Profiles updated, share firm activity on LinkedIn, and represent the firm well.

Let's explore some of the obstacles you might encounter when working with LinkedIn, and what avenues are available to help.

Where did that go? How do I...?

LinkedIn changes its interface often—it's one of the reasons we decided this version of the book wouldn't contain any screenshots. Even as often as we do training and presentations on LinkedIn, we have to change screenshots almost every time in order to stay current. As a result, even if you are a regular LinkedIn user, you might have trouble finding a feature or function that LinkedIn moved without warning, or you might simply need help recalling how to do something if you haven't done it in a while.

In cases like these, we recommend checking out LinkedIn's help feature as the first stop. As we mentioned earlier in this book, you can find it under the Me tab in the top navigation bar on any page on LinkedIn. We use it frequently ourselves—it was used often while writing this book to double-check that things hadn't changed as we were writing.

I'm not the best writer; I don't like how my Profile reads now, but I don't know how to fix it.

Everyone has their strengths and weaknesses, and some of us are better writers than others. It can be especially difficult to write about yourself and to see what you're writing objectively, from the point of view of your target audience. There are a few things you can do here if you are running into a problem.

First, ask someone who knows you and your work well—your best client, a colleague in your law firm, a law school classmate—to read your Profile and to make suggestions for revisions.

Next, ask someone who knows you but isn't necessarily familiar with the details about what you do to read your Profile. This could be a spouse, sibling, or friend who isn't in the legal field. Extra points if they fall within your target audience, whether that's clients, referral sources, etc. Then ask them some questions to see whether, after reading your Profile, they understand the main points you are trying to make, and if they understand what you do and who you are trying to attract with your Profile. Adjust your Profile accordingly.

If you still need help, it may be time to find a writer who can work with you to develop a more effective Profile. If you do hire someone to help, we recommend that you work with someone who is familiar with lawyers and their ethical obligations.

It's hard for me to constantly come up with ideas for content to post on LinkedIn.

We get it. It isn't always easy to come up with new ideas. But keep in mind that you don't always have to create your own content. If you use LinkedIn regularly and follow lots of interesting people, you can share content that others have shared or created on LinkedIn simply by looking at your Feed. We also recommend setting aside some time regularly (Monthly? Quarterly?) to brainstorm and come up with several ideas that you can then use throughout the month or quarter.

We also recommend that you keep a running list of frequently asked questions; keep a notebook or file on your computer where you can jot down ideas or topics for posts or articles as they come to you. Use a web-clipping service such as Evernote (***https://ever-note.com/***) to save articles, podcasts, or blog posts from the Internet that might form the basis of a post or a Publisher article. If there is a news story about an issue within your area of practice, take advantage of that to create a post reminding your audience of the ways that they can avoid the same problems or the steps they need to take to protect themselves. Help your clients, colleagues or other connections by writing posts about them or sharing what they're doing to help them gain visibility (subject, as always to the ethics rules of your jurisdiction).

If all else fails and you find that you are not consistent in your LinkedIn activity because you're having trouble generating ideas, it might be time to get some marketing help, even on a limited basis, from someone who can help you generate those ideas, develop an editorial calendar, or translate what you're already doing in other arenas to LinkedIn.

I need help staying on track and using LinkedIn consistently.

Here again, you have options. One might be to get together with some friends or colleagues and create an accountability group or mastermind group to help you all stay on track with your LinkedIn activity. You might brainstorm ideas together, set up regular calls or meetings to share what your goals are for using LinkedIn and report back to one another about your progress to establish some accountability. Or give someone in your office permission to remind you on a regular basis to participate on LinkedIn. Add LinkedIn to your calendar and block out time for working on it weekly.

If you need even more help, you can hire a coach or consultant to help.

I haven't used LinkedIn for much more than accepting invitations in so long, it's overwhelming—I don't know where to start.

We hope that this book and our basic LinkedIn Action Plan provides some first steps and helps reduce the feeling of being overwhelmed by LinkedIn, but if you need even more help, see below for how we might be able to help you further.

I'd like all of the legal professionals in my firm to have a LinkedIn Profile and to use LinkedIn consistently, but I'm having difficulty getting everyone to comply.

We recommend that you draw up some guidelines for use of LinkedIn for your firm or organization, with instructions and expectations to give something for your legal professionals and staff to refer to. You can give them a copy of this book or get some LinkedIn training for the legal professionals in the firm. For example, you might direct them to some of the services and resources below.

How We Can Help

We recognize that you're busy and that you don't have as much time to devote to LinkedIn, rooting around to learn about new features and how they work, experimenting with different strategies and techniques, and developing a consistent presence on LinkedIn. That's why, in addition to this book, we are continuing to develop other resources to help legal professionals use LinkedIn more effectively. If you need help, we have the following services and courses available:

Making LinkedIn Work for You Online Course

As this book goes to publication, we are working on developing this online course, following the structure of this book, to provide lawyers and other legal professionals with additional LinkedIn help. We'll go through much of what is discussed in the book, but we'll also share more of our personal experience and perspectives through short videos and will provide additional resources, such as worksheets and exercises, to help deepen your understanding and get you taking action.

Speaking, Webinars and Workshops

In addition to the online course, we are both available—either together or separately—to speak to your firm or organization about LinkedIn and how to use it effectively. We can provide workshops and webinars customized to your organization's needs and your members' familiarity with LinkedIn.

Group or Individual LinkedIn Training and Coaching

We can also provide you with hands-on LinkedIn training and coaching, either in groups or in an individual setting, in person or virtually through webinars or screen-sharing platforms. Grace Kennedy helps and coaches students, recent graduates, and other professionals, especially women and those in the LGBTQ+ community on improving their Profiles, their LinkedIn presence, and their LinkedIn strategies. (Reach out to Grace via LinkedIn at *linkedin.com/in/gkennedy1.*)

LinkedIn Copywriting Services

Allison helps her clients create or revise their LinkedIn Profiles to reach their target audience, incorporate their most important key-words, and craft a LinkedIn presence that helps them reach their goals for LinkedIn.

If you're interested in any of the above services,
you can contact us at:

DENNIS KENNEDY
dmk@denniskennedy.com
Phone: 734-926-5197
DennisKennedy.com

ALLISON C. SHIELDS
Allison@LegalEaseConsulting.com
Phone: 631-642-0221
LawyerMeltdown.com
LegalEaseConsulting.com (blog)

Made in the USA
Middletown, DE
31 January 2021

32829311R00156